Advancing Quantitative Methods in Criminology and Criminal Justice

Advancing Quantitative Methods in Criminology and Criminal Justice is designed to promote the understanding of various quantitative research methods and to encourage their use among those seeking answers to questions about crime and justice. To this end a number of top scholars have been assembled to provide their insights on a variety of 'cutting edge' quantitative research techniques. A wide range of expert contributors delve into the state of quantitative methods in the discipline, group-based trajectory modeling, spatial dependence models, structural equation models, meta-analysis, social network designs, panel data modeling, and censored regression techniques. This book will be highly beneficial for readers who seek to stay as current as possible as they pursue answers to questions about crime and justice using quantitative research methods.

This book was originally published as a special issue of the *Journal of Criminal Justice Education*.

Travis C. Pratt is a Professor in the School of Criminology and Criminal Justice at Arizona State University, USA. He is the author of more than forty-five refereed articles which have appeared in journals such as *Criminology, Justice Quarterly, Crime and Delinquency,* the *Journal of Research in Crime and Delinquency, Advances in Criminological Theory,* and *Crime and Justice: An Annual Review*. He is also the author of *Addicted to Incarceration: Corrections Policy and the Politics of Misinformation in the United States* (2009).

Advancing Quantitative Methods in Criminology and Criminal Justice

Edited by
Travis C. Pratt

Routledge
Taylor & Francis Group
LONDON AND NEW YORK

First published 2012
by Routledge
4 Park Square, Milton Park, Abingdon, Oxon OX14 4RN
605 Third Avenue, New York, NY 10017

Routledge is an imprint of the Taylor & Francis Group, an informa business

This book is a reproduction of the *Journal of Criminal Justice Education*, Volume 21, Issue 2. The Publisher requests to those authors who may be citing this book to state, also, the bibliographical details of the special issue on which the book was based.

British Library Cataloguing in Publication Data
A catalogue record for this book is available from the British Library

ISBN13: 978-0-415-78310-1 (hbk)

Typeset in Helvetica
by Taylor & Francis Books

Disclaimer
The publisher would like to make readers aware that the chapters in this book are referred to as articles as they had been in the special issue. The publisher accepts responsibility for any inconsistencies that may have arisen in the course of preparing this volume for print.

Contents

Notes on Contributors

Robert J. Fornango is an Assistant Professor in the School of Criminology & Criminal Justice at Arizona State University, USA. His research explores the dynamic processes that shape crime trends in the USA at the national, regional, city, and neighborhood levels. Specifically, his interests include studying the influences of structural change, criminal justice policies, and spatial dynamics in explaining social organization and violent crime. Recent co-authored work has appeared in the journals *Criminology* and *Criminology & Public Policy*.

Jacinta M. Gau is an Assistant Professor at the University of Central Florida, USA. Her research interests are primarily in the field of policing and include broken windows theory and order maintenance policing, race and policing, procedural justice and police–community relationships, and police use of force. Her work has appeared in journals such as *Justice Quarterly*, *Criminology & Public Policy*, *Police Quarterly*, and *Policing: An International Journal of Police Strategies and Management*.

David Kirk is an Assistant Professor in the Department of Sociology and a faculty research associate of the Population Research Center at the University of Texas at Austin, USA. His current research explores the influence of social context and neighborhood change on criminal behavior. Dr. Kirk's recent research has appeared in *American Sociological Review*, *Criminology*, *Demography*, and the *Journal of Quantitative Criminology*.

Tara Livelsberger is a doctoral student in the School of Criminal Justice at the University of Cincinnati, USA. She earned her MA in sociology at Ohio University in 2009. Her research interests include corrections, punishment and society, and research problems in criminology.

Jean Marie McGloin is an Associate Professor at the University of Maryland, USA, in the Department of Criminology and Criminal Justice. Her research interests include groups and crime, as well as specialization. Dr. McGloin's recent publications have appeared in *Criminology*, *the Journal of Quantitative Criminology*, and the *Journal of Research in Crime & Delinquency*.

Daniel S. Nagin is Teresa and H. John Heinz III University Professor of Public Policy and Statistics in the Heinz College, Carnegie Mellon University, USA. He is an elected fellow of the American Society of Criminology and of the American Society for the Advancement of Science, and is the 2006 recipient of the American Society of Criminology's Edwin H Sutherland Award. His research focuses on the evolution of criminal and antisocial behaviors over the life course, the deterrent effect of criminal and non-criminal penalties on illegal behaviors, and the development of statistical methods for analyzing longitudinal data.

Alex R. Piquero is a Professor of Criminology at the University of Texas at Dallas, USA, and co-editor of the *Journal of Quantitative Criminology*. His research interests include criminal careers, quantitative research methods, and criminological theory. He has received numerous research, teaching, and mentoring awards throughout his career.

Travis C. Pratt is a Professor in the School of Criminology and Criminal Justice at Arizona State University, USA. His research focuses on criminological theory and correctional policy, and he is the author of *Addicted to Incarceration: Corrections Policy and the Politics of Misinformation in the United States* (2009). His works have also appeared in *Crime and Justice: A Review of Research*, *Criminology*, *Journal of Research in Crime & Delinquency*, and *Justice Quarterly*.

Christopher J. Sullivan, PhD, is an Assistant Professor of Criminal Justice at the University of Cincinnati, USA. His research interests include developmental criminology; juvenile delinquency and prevention policy; and research and analytic methods. His recent work has appeared in *Criminology*, *Journal of Research in Crime & Delinquency*, *British Journal of Criminology*, and the *Journal of Quantitative Criminology*.

John L. Worrall is a Professor of Criminology at the University of Texas at Dallas, USA. He has published articles and book chapters on a wide range of topics ranging from legal issues in policing to community prosecution. He is also the author of *Crime Control in America: What Works?* (2nd ed., 2008) and *Criminal Procedure: From First Contact to Appeal* (3rd ed., 2010), co-author of *Policing Today* (2010), and co-editor of *The Changing Role of the American Prosecutor* (2009). He is also editor of the journal *Police Quarterly*.

INTRODUCTION

There has long been a power struggle between quantitative and qualitative approaches to criminal justice and criminological research (DiCristina 1997). While this debate is certainly not limited to our discipline, it has certainly infected it. Indeed, opposing camps have emerged, with fierce loyalties and allegiances to their own peer-reviewed journals, and terms like "quantoids"—a label that is meant to be both pejorative and a badge of honor depending upon which side one is on—have even been coined (Worrall 2000).

The qualitative-quantitative dichotomy strikes many as, at best, an empty debate and, at worst, utterly foolish—much like debating whether a hammer or a monkeywrench is "better." These methods are, after all, merely tools to help social scientists understand the world around them, nothing more. Nevertheless, real or not, the debate concerning which approach is superior has become real in its consequences as the quantitative approach has gained the upper hand in the discipline (Tewksbury, DeMichele, and Miller 2005). Value judgments aside, therefore, understanding these various methods takes on added importance for scholars in the field if they want their work to survive the peer review process.

The problem is that new quantitative methods tend to be developed at a pace that is far more rapid than the evolution of graduate curricula. Indeed, new techniques can be developed and spread throughout the discipline far faster than the administrative labyrinth of university curriculum changes can be navigated. In short, it's difficult for scholars to "keep up" if staying current means learning these techniques in the graduate classroom.

And while published work on various methodological topics can always be found in the peer-reviewed literature, much of this work is long on technical merit but short on context. That is where this special issue of the *Journal of Criminal Justice Education* comes in. The purpose of this collection of articles is to discuss some of the contemporary quantitative methods being used in the field in a way that would not be intended to replace the primary sources on these subjects, but rather to augment them in a way that scholars getting ready to cut their teeth with these methods may wish to consult first.

To that end, the articles that have been compiled in this issue have been written by some of the leading scholars in the discipline when it comes to the use and application of these various methods. These pieces are intended to present an overview of a number of techniques that are prevalent in the leading journals, yet for which many in the field may have little or no formal training, let alone first-hand experience with using. They run the spectrum substantively from relatively well-established techniques to those that are beginning to become more common to those that are likely to be used more and more in the future. And while some articles contain more technical detail while others are more broad-based, they all share the same approach of making these techniques accessible to a wider audience than has perhaps been reached thus far. To that end, we all hope you enjoy the issue and find it useful for your work in the future.

References

DiCristina, B. 1997. The quantitative emphasis in criminal justice education. *Journal of Criminal Justice Education* 8: 181–200.

Tewksbury, R., M. T. DeMichele, and J. M. Miller. 2005. Methodological orientations of articles appearing in criminal justice's top journals: Who publishes what and where. *Journal of Criminal Justice Education* 16: 265–279.

Worrall, J. L. 2000. In defense of the "quantoids:" More on the reasons for the quantitative emphasis in criminal justice education and research. *Journal of Criminal Justice Education* 11: 353-362.

Travis C. Pratt

Using the Group-Based Trajectory Model to Study Crime Over the Life Course

Daniel S. Nagin and Alex R. Piquero

Recognizing that social, behavioral, and biological processes evolve over time, criminologists have been interested in how the phenomenon of crime changes over time and thus have paid close attention to developmental trajectories of crime. Several research methodologies and statistical techniques have been developed to permit study of developmental trajectories. This paper provides a non-technical overview of a method developed to examine behavioral changes over age or time—group-based trajectory modeling (GBTM). Following background material, we provide an overview of the technique. This is followed by a discussion of the applicability of the method to a variety of criminological questions, a brief review of the existing applications of the method, including the software used, as well as the advantages and disadvantages of the trajectory approach for particular questions. The paper concludes with an outline of methodological and substantive "next-steps" regarding GBTM and its application in criminology and criminal justice research.

Introduction

All social, behavioral, and biological processes evolve over time (Nagin 2005, p. 1). Criminologists are specifically interested in questions about how the phenomenon of crime changes over time. For example, is there variation in the crime rate across and/or between large cities over time? Is there variation in the crime rate across and/or between persons over time? Do personality characteristics change over time? What all these three questions have in common is their focus on how a specific behavior changes over age or time. At the level of the individual, the course of an outcome or behavior over age or time is commonly referred to as a developmental trajectory. A number of research methodologies and statistical techniques have been developed to permit study of developmental trajectories. This paper provides a non-technical overview of one particular method that was expressly developed to examine behavioral changes over age or time—group-based trajectory modeling (GBTM).

We begin by providing background information on the development of GBTM and then turn our attention to a brief non-technical overview of the technique. This is followed by a discussion of the applicability of the method to a variety of criminological questions, a brief review of the existing applications of the method, including the software used, as well as the advantages and disadvantages of the trajectory approach for particular questions. The paper concludes with an outline of methodological and substantive "next-steps" regarding GBTM and its application in criminology and criminal justice research.

Background

The origins of the development of the GBTM are located in the voluminous criminal career literature, which has examined patterns of offending over the life course. Although early research in this area emerged from qualitative studies, criminal career research gained momentum with publication of Wolfgang, Figlio, and Sellin's (1972) seminal work *Delinquency in a Birth Cohort*. Studying the criminal activity of a birth cohort of 9,945 males born in Philadelphia in 1945 until they reached age 18, this study yielded the important finding that a small number of individuals (~6%) in the full birth cohort were responsible for over half of the crime. Further, there were notable differences regarding the offending patterns among cohort members, as most individuals who had a single official police contact did not register a second one, and among those who had two official police contacts, an even fewer proportion incurred a third official police contact, and so forth. Subsequently replicated in many other longitudinal studies, this pattern of findings highlights the variation that exists within the population of offenders, some offend rarely, some offend for some period of time and then desist, and others offend at a high-rate for a long period of time (Blumstein, Cohen, Roth, and Visher 1986; Piquero, Farrington, and Blumstein 2003).

The findings underscoring the heterogeneity among offenders spurred the development of several new theoretical frameworks seeking to further understand the longitudinal nature of criminal activity. One in particular, Moffitt's (1993) developmental taxonomy, hypothesized that two groups of offenders combined to form the aggregate representation of the age/crime curve. Life-course-persistent offenders are believed to represent a very small proportion of the offending population who exhibit early and serious antisocial behavior that continues throughout adolescence and into adulthood. Among this small group of offenders, offending is caused by an interaction between neuropsychological impairment and deficient environmental circumstances which combine to form an antisocial personality structure that is highly stable over the life course. For these individuals, change is unusual and negative behaviors permeate all facets of their lives. On the other hand, adolescence-limited offenders engage in acts that resemble adult-like status, including underage drinking and drug use, vandalism, theft, and precocious sexual activity, because these individuals are caught in a maturity gap—biologically capable of being adults yet prohibited from doing so because of their age. Individuals in this group seek out the aid and comfort of the peer social context, i.e., individuals like themselves, and engage in group-oriented behaviors designed to alleviate their perceived strain. This larger group of offenders does not sustain their involvement with crime beyond adolescence because they are not impaired by an injurious childhood and neuropsychological deficits that are characteristic of life-course persistent offenders. For them, change is the norm and entrance into early adulthood evinces a virtual cessation from crime. Review of the empirical record of this and other theories may be found in Farrington (2003) and Moffitt (2006).

Taken together, extant developmental theories and empirical research raise the possibility of important variation underlying longitudinal crime patterns. Yet, most statistical approaches for analyzing longitudinal data (developmental trajectories) are designed to account for individual variability about a mean population trend, and thus ignore the possibility that there are meaningful subgroups within a population that follow distinct developmental trajectories that are not identifiable ex ante (Nagin 2005, p. 1). Thus, it becomes necessary to have a methodological approach that permits detection and examination of individuals following distinctive developmental trajectories. Group-based trajectory is designed to provide just this capability for identifying distinctive developmental trajectories in time- and age-based data. The next section describes this approach in further detail.

The Group-Based Trajectory Modeling

Unlike approaches that assume the existence of trajectories before statistical analysis or make subjective assessments about such trajectories, GBTM provides the capacity for testing whether the hypothesized trajectories emerge from the data itself and further provides an exploratory capacity to identify previously unrecognized developmental patterns. In short, GBTM is specifically and statistically designed to examine processes that evolve over age or time.

GBTM was first demonstrated in Nagin and Land (1993). Their aim was to develop a modeling strategy that makes no parametric assumptions about the distribution of developmental trajectories in the population. Instead the distribution is approximated by a finite number of groups. Each category within the multinomial mixture can be viewed as a point of support, or grouping, for the distribution of individual-level trajectories. The model, then, estimates a separate point of support (or grouping) for as many distinct groups that are identified in the data.

Because the trajectory groups approximate population differences in developmental trajectories, a higher number of points of support (groups) yields a discrete distribution that more closely approximates what may be a true continuous distribution (Nagin and Tremblay 2005a). As originally reported in Nagin and Land (1993, p. 339, figure 1), Figure 1 displays two panels. The first panel,

(A), depicts the population distribution of some behavior, z, while the second panel, (B), replicates the same distribution but is overlaid with a histogram that approximates its shape. Panel B illustrates that any continuous distribution with finite end-points can be approximated by a discrete distribution (a histogram) or alternatively by a finite number of "points of support" (Nagin and Tremblay 2005a). A higher number of points of support yield a discrete distribution that more closely approximates what may be a true continuous distribution (Nagin and Tremblay 2005a).

Further, because each individual has a non-zero probability of belonging to each of the various groups identified, s/he can be assigned to the group to which s/he has the highest probability of belonging to. This is an important feature of the method because it permits researchers to assess the claims of developmental theories, such as Moffitt's, that make predictions about distinct offender groups. The GBTM developed by Nagin and Land has three additional features that make it useful in studying developmental trajectories. First, it has the flexibility to model data according to a number of different types of distributions, including the Poisson, the zero-inflated Poisson, the Bernoulli, and the censored normal. The censored normal distribution is useful for modeling longitudinal measurements of psychometric scale data such as for physical aggression; the Poisson and the zero-inflated Poisson distributions are useful for modeling longitudinal count data such as arrest histories; and the Bernoulli

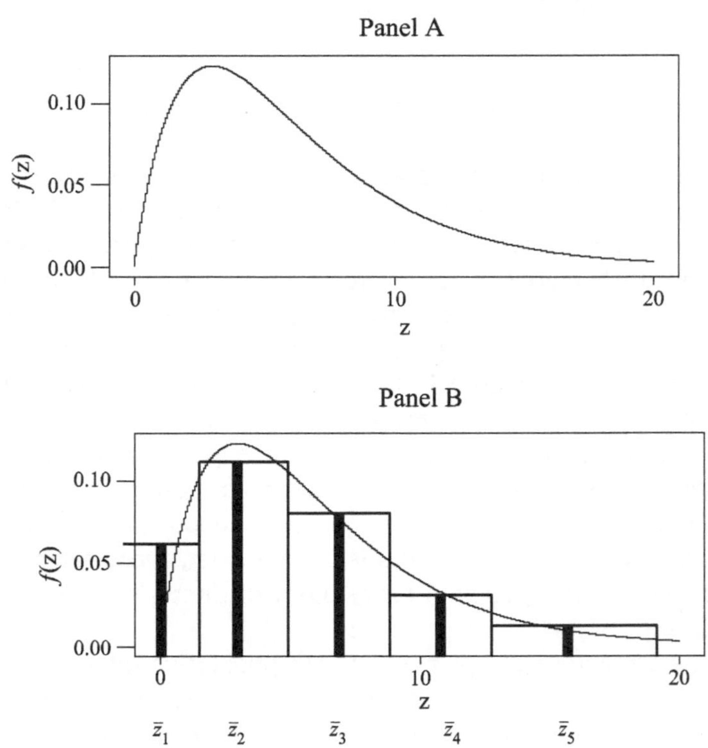

Figure 1 Using groups to approximate an unknown distribution.

distribution is useful for modeling longitudinal dichotomous data such as annual data on gang membership status. This is important because crime is measured in many different ways and these estimators permit examining them in the most appropriate manner. Second, the zero-inflated Poisson version of the model takes into account periods of non-offending, or intermittency. Third, the GBTM is more systematic in the way it categorizes offenders because it identifies distinctive groups by applying a formal, objective statistical criterion as opposed to a subjective classification. This makes GBTM well-suited for research problems with a taxonomic dimension whose aim is to chart out distinct developmental trajectories, to understand what factors account for their distinctiveness, and to test whether individuals following different trajectories also respond differently to an intervention (Nagin and Tremblay 2005a).[1]

Trajectories are Not the Only Approach

The GBTM is not the only approach for studying the developmental course of individual-level criminality. Other approaches, such as hierarchical and latent growth curve modeling, are also available. A key difference between GBTM and these other models is that the latter treat the population distribution of criminal activity as continuous whereas GBTM approximates this continuous distribution with points of support, or groups. GBTM, then, is designed to identify distinct, developmental trajectories within the population, to calibrate the probability of population members following each such trajectory, and to relate those probabilities to covariates of interest (Nagin 1999, p. 153).

Raudenbush (2001, p. 59) provides a useful description of the various methods and the questions they seek to address: "In many studies of growth it is reasonable to assume that all participants are growing according to some common function but that the growth parameters vary in magnitude." He offered children's vocabulary growth curves as an example of such a growth process. Two distinctive features of such developmental processes are: (1) they are generally monotonic—thus, the term *growth*, and (2) they vary regularly within the population. For such processes it is natural to ask, "What is the typical pattern of growth within the population and how does this typical growth pattern vary across population members?" Hierarchical and latent curve modeling are specifically designed to answer such a question. Raudenbush also

1. Trajectory-based methods lend themselves to the presentation of findings in the form of easily understood graphical and tabular data summaries (Nagin 2005, p. 3), and the output from the method serves many useful functions. First, after sorting individuals into the trajectories, researchers can treat the groups as categories and examine how risk/protective factors vary across the groups. This classify/analyze approach provides basic description about how the various trajectories differ along key variables. Second, the trajectories can be used as outcome variables in a multinomial logistic regression framework, where independent variables predict membership in the groups. A third function is the use of the group classifications as predictors in a regression-based framework. This approach allows for an examination of how certain variables relate to outcomes after considering unobserved individual differences measured via trajectories.

offered an example of a developmental process—depression—that does not generally change monotonically over time and does not vary regularly through the population, and observed (p. 59), "It makes no sense to assume that everyone is increasing (or decreasing) in depression ... many persons will never be high in depression, others will always be high; some are recovering from serious depression, while others will become increasingly depressed." For these sorts of problems, he recommended the use of a multinomial-type method because modeled trajectories vary regularly across population members. Indeed, some trajectories vary greatly across population subgroups both in terms of the level of behavior at the outset of the measurement period and in the rate of growth and decline over time. According to Raudenbush (2001, p. 60), GBTM is "especially useful when trajectories of change involve sets of parameters that mark qualitatively different kinds of development." For such problems, a modeling strategy designed to identify averages and explain variability about that average is far less useful than a trajectory approach designed to identify distinct clusters of trajectories and to calibrate how characteristics of individuals and their circumstances affect membership in these trajectories (Raudenbush 2001, p. 60).

Limitations of GBTM

All statistical methods have limitations and GBTM is not an exception. First, the identification of parameter estimates is difficult with a small set of observation periods and where the prevalence of observations is also small. Second, classification of individuals to distinct trajectories will never be perfect (Roeder, Lynch, and Nagin 1999). Third, the number of groups extracted is variable and partly a function of sample size—the more individuals the more groups one is likely to find (Nagin and Tremblay 2001, p. 30).[2] Still, the number of groups appears to plateau at a sample size of about 200, and the conclusions reached about the number of groups above this sample size do not vary much (D'Unger, Land, McCall, and Nagin 1998). Fourth, Eggleston, Laub, and Sampson (2004) identified three data-related features that influence trajectories including: length of follow-up, inclusion of incarceration time, and involuntary desistance through death.[3] Their analysis indicated that follow-up length can influence group shape, peak ages, and group membership, and that length is most relevant for high-rate offenders who continue offending into adulthood. Fifth, excluding incarceration time results in underestimating the rate of offending and can affect group shape, peak age, and group membership, and appears most relevant for high-rate offenders (Piquero et al. 2001) and the high-rate chronic group is greatly affected by the

2. If the underlying distribution is indeed discrete and not continuous, then an increase in sample size will not artificially lead to an increase in the number of groups identified.

3. These data-related features also affect the conclusions drawn from non-GBTM approaches.

exclusion of mortality data, primarily because those who are dead are assumed to have desisted.

A final but important concern is that the GBTM is vulnerable to misappropriation by those pre-disposed to believe in the idea of certain types of offenders (Sampson, Laub, and Eggleston 2004). Nagin and Tremblay (2005a, 2005b) concur and observe that there has been confusion about the interpretation of the model, stemming primarily from the interpretation of what it means to say "person *x* belongs to trajectory group *j*." Three misconceptions in particular were identified: individuals actually belong to a trajectory group, the number of trajectory groups in a sample is immutable, and the trajectories of group members follow the group-level trajectory in lockstep (Nagin and Tremblay 2005a). With regard to the first caution, there has always been a caution against group reification. Regarding the second caution, the groups are intended as an approximation (i.e., not fixed) of a more complex underlying reality primarily because longitudinal data are limited not only by the number of individuals but also by the number of periods or sets of observations for which individuals are observed. As more periods of data are added, trajectories may vary. As Nagin and Tremblay (2005a) point out, "more data allows for more refined statistical inferences." Finally, because GBTM creates a summary that describes the behavior and characteristics of individuals following similar developmental courses (i.e., it summarizes the average behavioral trend of a collection of individuals), individuals assigned to specific trajectories may not follow the overall trajectory pattern perfectly. In other words, it is not the case that all individuals in a trajectory group will follow that trajectory in lockstep, only that individuals assigned to a particular trajectory resemble one another and the overall trajectory moreso than they do another trajectory. A group within the trajectory context is a cluster of approximately homogenous individuals in the sense that they are following about the same developmental course, and have distinct characteristics from other clusters of individuals following different developmental courses (Nagin and Tremblay 2005a).[4] The cautions remain: individuals do not actually belong to a trajectory group; the number of trajectory groups in a sample is not immutable; and individuals do not follow the group-level trajectory in lockstep.

Software

Currently, software and documentation to employ GBTM through the SAS platform is available at http://www.andrew.cmu.edu/user/bjones/. Jones,

4. It is important to bear in mind that the variation within the trajectory is random variation conditional on trajectory (group) membership, while the variation between the trajectories is structural. Still, B. Muthén (personal communication, 24 January 2007) argues that GBTM does indeed assume that individuals belong to a trajectory group. He indicates that to the extent that GBTM views this as merely an approximation, then researchers should use a growth mixture model where within-class variation is allowed.

Nagin, and Roeder (2001) and Jones and Nagin (2007) outlined the use of the software in an accessible manner, and the online documentation walks readers through the entire process from data construction to model building to model interpretation. Additionally, other statistical applications, such as LATENT GOLD and M-PLUS, also perform trajectory estimations, and other researchers have developed methods for GBTM (Muthén 2004; Muthén and Muthén 2000).

Applications of GBTM

GBTM has been widely applied in the social sciences with applications to diverse topics such as internet use, the development of obesity, trajectories of crime in geographic units, and well over 80 studies on antisocial and criminal activity (see review in Piquero 2008). Here, we provide several examples of how GBTM has been applied to study interesting questions in criminology.

We begin with a trajectory-based analysis of the offending careers of a historical sample of delinquent Boston males originally collected by the Gluecks and then followed-up with an official arrest record search to age 70. Sampson and Laub (2003, p. 582, figure 11) identified six distinct trajectories. Three points are in order regarding the trajectories: (1) a small group (~3.2%) were labeled as "high-rate chronics," whose offending activity peaked in the late 30s, and then dropped close to zero by age 60; (2) three other trajectory groups peaked in middle adolescence, late adolescence, and early adulthood, respectively, and then began a slow decline toward zero in adulthood; and (3) a small group (~8%) "low-rate chronics," had a steady offending trajectory between the ages of 19 and 39, at which point their offending began to decline.[5] Additionally, when they compared selected childhood and adolescent risk factors across trajectory groups, inconsistent patterns emerged with no significant differences in means across the six groups of offending (for total crime), though the results indicated that the (very small) high-rate chronic group had the worst risk factors.

In our second example, we review a study by Bushway, Thornberry, and Krohn (2003) who applied GBTM to self-report data from the Rochester Youth Development Study to examine issues related to desistance. Following their subjects from age 13.5 to 22, these authors examined whether conclusions regarding desistance would vary according to two definitions of desistance: (1) a "static" definition which classifies as desisters those individuals who offended at least once before age 18, but not afterward (through age 22; 27.6% of the sample met this desister definition), and (2) a "developmental" definition which is based on GBTM which not only indicates which individuals approach a

5. Controlling for exposure time through age 32 identified only five groups, but the predicted number of offenses was much higher with exposure time data. Still, by age 32, the offending patterns in the exposure time analysis appeared to diminish.

zero rate of offending, but also provides information regarding how long they have been there. Seven distinct trajectories were identified in their study, two of which approximated individuals who looked like they had desisted (Bushway et al. 2003, p. 144, figure 1). After further consideration, the authors decided that only one of these groups (8.4% of the sample) fit their definition of desistance, i.e., "experienced real change ... and [provided] no evidence [of] an upswing of offending at the end of the period" (Bushway et al. 2003, pp. 143-144). Of the 291 individuals identified as desisters by the two methods, there was agreement in only 4.8% of the cases.

Our third example moves beyond descriptions of longitudinal offending trajectories and follows a suggestion made by Nagin (2005) in linking the group-based trajectories to non-crime outcomes. Piquero, Farrington, Nagin, and Moffitt (2010) used previously identified trajectories of criminal activity through age 40 for the 411 South London males who participated in the Cambridge Study in Delinquent Development (Piquero, Farrington, and Blumstein 2007) in order to predict life failure at age 48 (i.e., unemployment, poor mental health, etc.). They found differential effects for offending trajectories on life failure measure. Further, higher-rate chronic offenders exhibited more life failure than other offenders—even after controlling for early-life risk factors, while shorter-term lower-level offenders and non-offenders were leading the most successful lives.

Of course there are many other examples and applications of GBTM but space constraints limit our review here. Still, we close with a brief description of a very unique analysis that is permittable with GBTM and concerns the possibility of path dependencies in the response to a turning point such as marriage or treatments such as hospitalization for a psychiatric disorder (Nagin 2005, p. 9). In this application of GBTM, Nagin, Pagani, Tremblay, and Vitaro (2003) found that the impact of grade retention on physical aggression depended upon the child's trajectory of physical aggression. The subsequent physical aggression of children who had been following trajectories of little physical aggression or of chronic physical aggression appeared to be unaffected by the event of being held back in school. By contrast, the physical aggression of individuals who had been following trajectories of declining physical aggression seemed to be exacerbated.

Future Directions in GBTM and Research

The purpose of this paper has been to provide an overview of a particular methodological approach for studying phenomena that change over time. We have attempted to provide a non-technical overview of GBTM, its principle advantages and disadvantages, and highlighted several applications of it to criminological questions. We believe that the method offers criminologists one important tool for the longitudinal study of crime phenomena, and one that offers some unique insight unavailable through other methodological and statistical techniques. As Nagin (2005, pp. 1-2) observes, GBTM's feature of charting out distinct trajectories is especially suitable for "research problems with a taxonomic [i.e., developmental] dimension ... to understand what factors account for their distinctiveness, and to test whether individuals following the different trajectories also respond differently to a treatment such as a medical intervention or to a major life event such as the birth of a child." At the same time, there is much room for further application of GBTM in criminology. Some examples include studying changes in self-control and involvement with delinquent peers with age, analyzing the "co-morbidity" of trajectories based on official records with those based on self reports using dual trajectory modeling (Brame, Mulvey, and Piquero 2001; Nagin 2005; Nagin and Tremblay 2001), unpacking the group and looking at individual variation, and applying the causal inferences methods laid out in Haviland, Nagin, and Rosenbaum (2007) and Haviland and Nagin (2005) that combine propensity score matching and trajectory modeling to more criminological applications. Also, more methodological work such as that in Brame, Nagin, and Wasserman (2006) for testing model fit and properties is very desirable.

Acknowledgments

This manuscript borrows material from Piquero (2008), and we would like to thank Springer Publishing for permission to reproduce some of this material. This work was funded in part by the National Science Foundation (NSF) (SES-99113700; SES-0647576).

References

Blumstein, A., J. Cohen, J. A. Roth, and C. A. Visher (Eds.). 1986. *Criminal careers and career criminals*. Washington, DC: National Academy Press.

Brame, R., E. P. Mulvey, and A. R. Piquero. 2001. On the development of different kinds of criminal activity. *Sociological Methods and Research* 29: 319-341.

Brame, R., D. S. Nagin, and L. Wasserman. 2006. Exploring some analytical characteristics of finite mixture models. *Journal of Quantitative Criminology* 22: 31-59.

Bushway, S. D., T. P. Thornberry, and M. D. Krohn. 2003. Desistance as a developmental process: A comparison of static and dynamic approaches. *Journal of Quantitative Criminology* 19: 129-153.

D'Unger, A. V., K. C. Land, P. L. McCall, and D. S. Nagin. 1998. How many latent classes of delinquent/criminal careers? Results from mixed Poisson regression analyses of the London, Philadelphia, and Racine cohort studies. *American Journal of Sociology* 103: 1593-1630.

Eggleston, E. P., J. H. Laub, and R. J. Sampson. 2004. Methodological sensitivities to latent class analysis of long-term criminal trajectories. *Journal of Quantitative Criminology* 20: 1-26.

Farrington, D. P. 2003. Developmental and life-course criminology: Key theoretical and empirical issues—the 2002 Sutherland Award Address. *Criminology* 41: 221-255.

Haviland, A. M., and D. S. Nagin. 2005. Causal inferences with group based trajectory models. *Psychometrika* 70: 557-578.

Haviland, A. M., D. S. Nagin, and P. R. Rosenbaum. 2007. Combining propensity score matching and group-based trajectory modeling in an observational study. *Psychological Methods* 12: 247-267.

Jones, B. L., and D. S. Nagin. 2007. Advances in group-based trajectory modeling and a SAS procedure for estimating them. *Sociological Methods and Research* 35: 542-572.

Jones, B. L., D. S. Nagin, and K. Roeder. 2001. A SAS procedure based on mixture models for estimating developmental trajectories. *Sociological Methods and Research* 29: 374-393.

Moffitt, T. E. 1993. "Life-course-persistent" and "adolescence-limited" antisocial behavior: A developmental taxonomy. *Psychological Review* 100: 674-701.

Moffitt, T. E. 2006. Life-course persistent versus adolescence-limited antisocial behavior. In D. Cicchetti and D. Cohen (Eds.), *Developmental psychopathology* (2nd ed., pp. 570-598). New York: Wiley.

Muthén, B. 2004. Latent variable analysis: Growth mixture modeling and related techniques for longitudinal data. In D. Kaplan (Ed.), *Handbook of quantitative methodology for the social sciences* (pp. 345-368). Newbury Park, CA: Sage.

Muthén, B., and L. Muthén. 2000. Integrating person-centered and variable-centered analysis: Growth mixture modeling with latent trajectory classes. *Alcoholism: Clinical and Experimental Research* 24: 882-891.

Nagin, D. S. 1999. Analyzing developmental trajectories: A semi-parametric, group-based approach. *Psychological Methods* 4: 139-177.

Nagin, D. S. 2005. *Group-based modeling of development over the life course*. Cambridge, MA: Harvard University Press.

Nagin, D. S., and K. C. Land. 1993. Age, criminal careers, and population heterogeneity: Specification and estimation of a nonparametric, mixed Poisson model. *Criminology* 31: 327-362.

Nagin, D. S., L. Pagani, R. E. Tremblay, and F. Vitaro. 2003. Life course turning points: A case study of the effect of school failure on interpersonal violence. *Development and Psychopathology* 15: 343-361.

Nagin, D. S., and R. E. Tremblay. 2001. Analyzing developmental trajectories of distinct but related behaviors: A group-based method. *Psychological Methods* 6: 18-34.

Nagin, D. S., and R. E. Tremblay. 2005a. Developmental trajectory groups: Fact of fiction? *Criminology* 43: 873-904.

Nagin, D. S., and R. E. Tremblay. 2005b. From seduction to passion: A response to Sampson and Laub. *Criminology* 43: 915-918.

Piquero, A. R. 2008. Taking stock of developmental trajectories of criminal activity over the life course. In A. Liberman (Ed.), *The long view of crime: A synthesis of longitudinal research* (pp. 23-78). New York: Springer.

Piquero, A. R., A. Blumstein, R. Brame, R. Haapenen, E. P. Mulvey, and D. S Nagin. 2001. Assessing the impact of exposure time and incapacitation on longitudinal trajectories of criminal offending. *Journal of Adolescent Research* 16: 54-74.

Piquero, A. R., D. P. Farrington, and A. Blumstein. 2003. The criminal career paradigm. In M. Tonry (Ed.), *Crime and justice: A review of research* (Vol. 30, pp. 359-506). Chicago: University of Chicago Press.

Piquero, A. R., D. P. Farrington, and A. Blumstein. 2007. *Key issues in criminal career research: New analyses of the Cambridge Study in Delinquent Development*. New York: Cambridge University Press.

Piquero, A. R., D. P. Farrington, D. S. Nagin, and T. E. Moffitt. 2010. Trajectories of offending and their relation to life failure in late middle age: Findings from the

Cambridge Study in Delinquent Development. *Journal of Research in Crime & Delinquency* 47 (2), forthcoming.

Raudenbush, S. 2001. Toward a coherent framework for comparing trajectories of individual change. In L. M. Collins and A. G. Sayer (Eds.), *New methods for the analysis of change* (pp. 35–64). Washington, DC: APA.

Roeder, K., K. Lynch, and D. S. Nagin. 1999. Modeling uncertainty in latent class membership: A case study in criminology. *Journal of the American Statistical Association* 94: 766–776.

Sampson, R. J., and J. H. Laub. 2003. Life-course desisters? Trajectories of crime among delinquent boys followed to age 70. *Criminology* 41: 555–592.

Sampson, R. J., J. H. Laub, and E. P. Eggleston. 2004. On the robustness and validity of groups. *Journal of Quantitative Criminology* 20: 37–42.

Wolfgang, M. E., R. M. Figlio, and T. Sellin. 1972. *Delinquency in a birth cohort*. Chicago: University of Chicago Press.

When Space Matters: Spatial Dependence, Diagnostics, and Regression Models

Robert J. Fornango

For researchers analyzing geographically oriented data, such as neighborhood or county crime rates, a serious threat to validity is the violation of OLS regression assumptions due to the spatial clustering of values for the variables in the analysis. In such circumstances, OLS regression estimates may be biased and inefficient. However, analytic methods for spatial data analysis allow formal assessments of spatial autocorrelation, as well as maximum likelihood spatial regression models. This paper presents discussions of the underlying logic of spatial effects, the impact of spatial dependence on non-spatial regression models, methods for assessing spatial dependence, the implementation of spatial regression models, and an illustration of the techniques presented. Additional discussion and references to more advanced spatial analytic techniques are provided.

Introduction

Recent developments in statistical computing software have opened the door to a class of models that are beginning to spread rapidly throughout criminology: spatial regression. While these techniques have been used effectively to study crime (Baller, Anselin, Messner, Deane, and Hawkins 2001; Griffiths and Chavez 2004; Mears and Bhati 2006), recidivism (Kubrin and Stewart 2006), gang activity (Cohen and Tita 1999; Rosenfeld, Bray, and Egley 1999), and collective efficacy (Morenoff and Sampson 1997; Morenoff, Sampson, and Raudenbush 2001), there remain a relatively small number of researchers making use of spatial data analysis techniques. Researchers using data sets pertaining to geographically contiguous entities, such as street blocks, neighborhoods, counties, and even states may not be making full use of the information contained in their data until potential spatial dependencies are examined, diagnosed, and addressed. Furthermore, regression coefficient results of spatially oriented data may be inefficient and biased unless appropriate steps are taken to account for the geographic structure of the observed units of analysis (Anselin 1988; Anselin and Bera 1998). The purpose of this paper is to (1) outline the underlying issues of spatial effects, (2) explain the impact spatial dependence has on non-spatial regression models, (3) present summary techniques for detecting spatial dependence, (4) offer guidance in determining the appropriate method to account for spatial dependence in regression models, and (5) present an empirical demonstration with freely available software.[1]

Spatial Effects: Underlying Processes

Spatial effects may take on two general forms: spatial dependence[2] and spatial heterogeneity (Anselin 1988). Spatial dependence refers to the most commonly conceptualized form of spatial effects, in which events in one location influence the events in other locations of a geographic system. These are sometimes thought of as contagion or diffusion effects (Cohen and Tita 1999). In the other form of spatial effect, spatial heterogeneity, the stability of relationships varies from one location in the system to another. This is most easily observed by a change in regression coefficients from one geographic region to another within a system, or spatially clustered heteroskedasticity. However, it should be noted that these two forms of spatial effects are not mutually exclusive situations. It is possible to have both spatial dependence and spatial heterogeneity present within the same data. For example, recent work by Baller et al. (2001) demonstrated that county level homicide rates in the USA exhibit spatial dependence, suggesting that the homicide rate in one county will have an influence on the homicide rate in neighboring counties. At the same time, regional differences in the relationships between independent and dependent variables existed between the northern and southern regions of the USA.

Spatial Heterogeneity and Spatial Dependence: Violations of OLS Assumptions

Both forms of spatial effects may violate assumptions of OLS regression (Anselin 1988). In the case of spatial heterogeneity, the error terms are unlikely to be homoskedastic or uncorrelated. Instead, the error variance is likely to differ across geographic regions, and be correlated within regions. Related to this problem, the estimated relationships (i.e., coefficients) are unlikely to be

1. This paper is intended to be an introductory reference for researchers interested in spatial data analysis. To that end, I restrict my general discussion to cross-sectional data analysis. More advanced techniques, discussed elsewhere, are available when estimating longitudinal or hierarchical models with spatial dependence. I will not discuss these techniques, but refer the reader to recent papers on the subject below. All examples presented are estimated using GeoDa statistical software, available at http://geodacenter.asu.edu/.

2. I will use the terms spatial dependence and spatial autocorrelation interchangeably throughout this text. However, it should be noted that spatial autocorrelation is a weaker form of strict spatial dependence.

linear across observations, differing by regions in the system. In the case of spatial dependence, since observations are correlated across geographic units, the OLS errors are likely to be correlated as well. Where such correlation is strong, errors terms for the entire system are unlikely to be homoskedastic or uncorrelated. Additionally, the linearity of relationships between independent and dependent variables may be jeopardized when spatial dependence is strong.

Defining Neighbors, Spatial Weights, and Spatial Lags

Before attempting to measure or diagnose issues of spatial dependence, researchers must first determine the relevant geographic structure of the data: what units will be considered "neighbors"? While there are many empirical techniques for choosing a relevant neighbor structure, this process should largely be informed by theoretical considerations. For example, studies examining crime rates across the neighborhoods of a city may consider the relevant neighbors of community *i* as only those communities sharing common boundaries. On the other hand, one may consider that neighborhoods are connected to a larger system of relationship networks throughout the city. Through such a perspective, one may conceive of a neighbor structure in which all communities of the city are related neighborhood *i*, but with influence inversely related to the geographic distance from *i*. The choice of appropriate neighbor structures will depend on the theoretically expected geographic connectivity of crime incidents in the city.

A number of techniques exist to define such structures, and can be illustrated using the hypothetical map in Figure 1. The simplest form is the contiguity matrix: an $N \times N$ matrix in which for each unit *i* (in the rows), all other *j* (in the columns) units receive a "1" if they share common border with unit *i*, and a "0" otherwise. For example, using rook contiguity the neighbors for unit *F* in Figure 1 would include units *B, E, G,* and *J* as they each share a common edge. Alternatively, queen contiguity considers neighbors to be units that share a common edge and vertex (Anselin 1988).[3] In Figure 1, the queen neighbors for unit *F* include units *A, B, C, E, G, I,* and *J*. A fourth method for conceptualizing neighbors is by using a distance band, usually extending from the centroid of a given geographical unit. In Figure 1, the dashed circle represents a distance band around unit *F*. Using this approximation, neighboring units are those whose centroids fall within the distance band around *F*, and include *B, E,* and *J*.

Neighbors are not always defined using a contiguity matrix. Instead they may be defined using a distance decay function in which all units are related to all others using the inverse distance, or negative exponentials of distance, between

3. Bishop contiguity is a third alternative to rook and queen contiguity in which neighbors are defined as those sharing a common vertex (Anselin 1988). However, in practice rook and bishop contiguity structures are used less often than queen contiguity definitions.

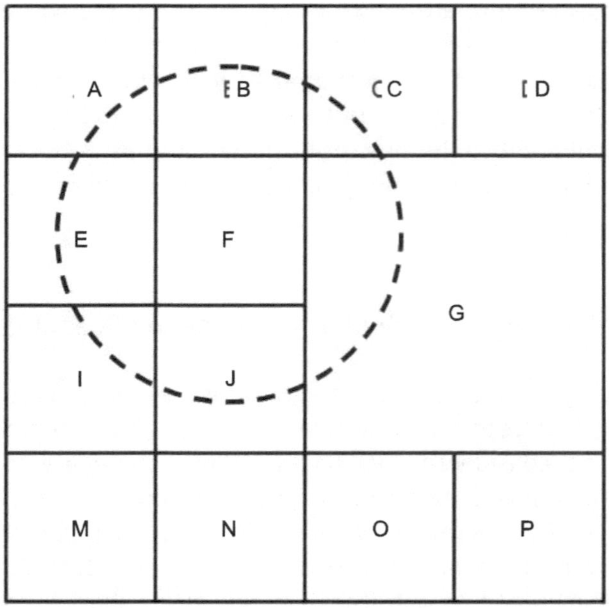

Figure 1 Neighbor classifications.

unit centroids (Cliff and Ord 1973, 1981). Using this conceptualization, units whose centroids are in closer proximity are given more weight than those with centroids farther away.

The use of a contiguity matrix definition may result in different numbers of neighbors for different units in the sample unless the number of neighbors is constrained to only using the *k*-th nearest neighbors. Therefore, the resulting contiguity matrix, *W*, will often be row-standardized so that the weights sum to 1 (Anselin 1988). However, when using inverse distance weights, row-standardization is often not used.

Assessment of Spatial Autocorrelation

Once the relevant neighbor structure has been defined, researchers may proceed with formal assessment of the degree of spatial relatedness present in the data. As a point of comparison, many are familiar with the concept of temporal autocorrelation present in time-series and panel data structures. Observations over time tend to be more highly correlated with temporally proximate values than those at more distant time points. In the case of spatial dependence, the null hypothesis is that the values of variable *X* are randomly distributed in geographic space. A rejection of this hypothesis implies that some form of spatial autocorrelation exists.

A number of statistics exist to measure the nature and strength of spatial autocorrelation. The most common global measure is Moran's *I*, which takes on a value of $-1/(n - 1)$ under the condition of a random spatial distribution, and takes on a range from −1 to +1 representing negative and positive spatial autocorrelation, respectively (Moran 1950; Ward and Gleditsch 2008). Moran's *I* may be calculated as:

$$I = \frac{n\sum_{i}\sum_{j\neq i} w_{ij}(x_i - \bar{x})(x_j - \bar{x})}{\left(\sum_{i}\sum_{j\neq i} w_{ij}\right)\sum_{i}(x_i - \bar{x})^2} \tag{1}$$

where *n* is the sample size, *x* is the variable of interest, and *w* are the elements of a row-standardized weights matrix.

If one substitutes the product sum in the numerator of *I* with the sum of squared differences, this measure becomes Geary's *C* (Geary 1954; Ward and Gleditsch 2008). Geary's *C* ranges in value from approximately 0 to 2. Values of 1 represent a condition of spatial randomness. Values above 1 represent negative autocorrelation and values below 1 represent positive autocorrelation, respectively.

$$C = \frac{n-1\sum_{i}\sum_{j\neq i} w_{ij}(x_i - x_j)^2}{2\left(\sum_{i}\sum_{j\neq i} w_{ij}\right)\sum_{i}(x_i - \bar{x})^2} \tag{2}$$

In this paper, I focus on Moran's *I* as a global measure of spatial autocorrelation due to its proliferation in both the literature and statistical software for spatial analysis.[4]

Assessment of Structural Similarity

When a phenomenon of interest exhibits non-zero correlation in space, it is relevant to consider the sources of spatial patterning. Generally speaking, the sources take one of four forms. First, the characteristics of areal units generating the phenomenon may cluster together in space thereby causing the outcome to cluster as well. This form of spatial process can be referred to as one of *structural similarity* (Baller et al. 2001). In determining if structural similarity is generating the spatial autocorrelation of the outcome, one may use an OLS

4. For alternative methods of assessing spatial autocorrelation, refer to Cliff and Ord (1973, 1981). Global measures of spatial autocorrelation such as Moran's *I* and Geary's *C* refer to the extent of spatial patterning for an entire system of areal units (i.e., a lattice system). See Cressie (1993) for methods appropriate for distance-based weights. Additionally, there are local indicators of spatial autocorrelation (LISA) that describe the contribution of each observation to the global measure (Anselin 1995; Getis and Ord 1992; Ord and Getis 1995).

regression model and examine the residuals for spatial autocorrelation using Moran's *I* (Anselin and Bera 1998). If structural similarity is ruled out through persistent spatial autocorrelation of the OLS residuals, then a spatial model should be considered. However, the researcher must determine the form of the spatial model to use. In the second form, the outcome itself may be partially generated by some form of contagion or diffusion process, thereby influencing the value of the outcome in neighboring units and is sometimes referred to as a *spatial effect* (Baller et al. 2001; Cohen and Tita 1999; Doreian 1980). A third source may be due to an omitted variable from the model, and the spatial dependence can be modeled as part of the error term. This may be referred to as a *spatial disturbance* (Baller et al. 2001; Doreian 1980). Anselin (1988) refers the spatial effect model as a *spatial lag model*, and the spatial disturbance model as a *spatial error model*, encompassing both under the general term *spatial dependence models*. A final form of spatial effect to consider is *spatial heterogeneity* in the form of regression parameter instability across space (Anselin 1988). When spatial heterogeneity is present, the structural form of the regression may differ from one region to another in the system, or the regression coefficients may differ. Additionally, spatial heterogeneity and spatial dependence may both be present in the data.

After estimation of an OLS model to assess the structural similarity of units, the residuals from the regression may be examined for spatial autocorrelation. Anselin and Bera (1998) provide a *z*-test for Moran's *I* of the residuals, based on approximating a normal distribution. If the *z*-test is significant, this is evidence that spatial autocorrelation in the dependent variable is not explained strictly by the structural characteristics of the units included in the OLS model. Under such circumstances, an alternative specification that explicitly accounts for the spatial structure of the data is necessary. However, additional diagnostic tests are required to determine an appropriate alternative.

Diagnostic Tests for Alternative Specifications

A series of Lagrange Multiplier (LM) tests may be used in deciding whether the appropriate spatial regression model should be a spatial lag or spatial error model (Anselin, Bera, Florax, and Yoon 1996; Anselin and Florax 1995). The LM test statistics are calculated using the residuals and parameter estimates from a non-spatial OLS regression model. Two different LM tests are available, one for each of the alternatives of a spatial lag and a spatial error (Anselin 1988; Anselin and Florax 1995). A significant LM-error test statistic indicates a preference for a spatial error model, while a significant LM-lag test indicates a preference for the spatial lag model. However, occasionally the LM-error and LM-lag tests will both be significant, making the correct alternative model unclear. Therefore, Anselin et al. (1996) have developed LM tests for spatial lags and spatial errors that are robust to the presence of the other alternative. When both standard LM tests are significant, the robust LM-lag and robust LM-error tests should be examined.

Spatial Lag Model and Spatial Error Models

The underlying logic of spatial dependence models can be derived from a general equation (Anselin 1988):

$$y = \rho Wy + X\beta + \varepsilon$$
$$\varepsilon = \lambda W\varepsilon + \mu \quad (3)$$

In Equation 3, *W* represents a spatial weights matrix defining neighboring units in space. The outcome *y* is a function of *Wy*, the weighted average of the outcome in neighboring units with the coefficient estimate ρ, a vector of exogenous independent variables *X* with the coefficient estimate β, and an error term ε. Additionally, the error term ε for the outcome *y* is a function of $W\varepsilon$, a weighted autoregressive term based on errors in neighboring units with the effect estimate λ, and a residual μ which is assumed to be independent across units, normally distributed, and homoskedastic.[5] Additionally, the two *W* are assumed to be equivalent.[6] Shown in its nested form, Equation 1 becomes:

$$y = \rho Wy + X\beta + (\lambda W\varepsilon + \mu) \quad (4)$$

In the generalized form of Equation 4, the two potential sources of spatial effects become clear. Spatial dependence exists if the parameter $\rho \neq 0$, and represents the influence of a spatially lagged dependent variable. Spatial error exists if the parameter $\lambda \neq 0$, and represents the spatially autoregressive error term. Additionally, Equation 4 illustrates that it is possible for both ρ and λ to be different from zero, such that both spatial dependence and spatial heterogeneity may exist in the same model. However, to make the utility of Equation 4 clearer consider the case where $\rho = \lambda = 0$. In this situation, Equation 4 reduces to the classic linear regression model:

$$y = X\beta + \mu \quad (5)$$

While Equation 5 illustrates that when $\rho = \lambda = 0$ in Equation 4 we have the classic linear regression model, when faced with evidence that either $\rho \neq 0$, $\lambda \neq 0$, or both, the researcher must determine the correct model specification to use. Therefore, it is useful to illustrate two variations on Equation 4. First, consider a spatial process in which $\lambda = 0$ and $\rho \neq 0$. In this scenario the outcome *y* is a

5. Technically, μ does not need to be homoskedastic. Anselin (1988) demonstrates spatial dependence models in which this assumption may be relaxed such that the error variance may be heteroskedastic. This would imply a situation of spatial heterogeneity, in which the structural model presented in Equation 1 may have different coefficient estimates across units in geographic space (see Anselin 1988; Baller et al. 2001). However, to simplify explanation here, I impose the assumption constant error variance.

6. Anselin (1988) demonstrates that the spatial weights matrix *W* for ρ does not need to be equivalent to the *W* for λ. As with the assumption of homoskedastic errors, I impose this restriction to ease illustration of the model. However in practice, the assumption that the *W* are equivalent is often implicitly made as researchers rarely use two different weight matrixes.

function of spatially lagged values of the neighboring y, and there is no direct spatial autoregressive function. Equation 4 thus reduces to:

$$y = \rho Wy + X\beta + \mu \quad (6)$$

In Equation 6, as in Equation 4, it is clear that y on the right side of the equation is not strictly exogenous. Rather, y for any given unit is explained as a function of y in neighboring locations, which in turn are explained by the y of their neighbors. This process continues throughout the geographic system such that the outcome for each unit has an influence on the outcome in every other unit with distance decay effects, also known as a spatial multiplier process (Anselin 1988; Anselin, Cohen, Cook, Gorr, and Tita 2000). To resolve this endogeneity, Equation 6 must be rewritten such that y is not present on the right side of the equation. In matrix form, we obtain:

$$\begin{aligned} y - \rho Wy &= X\beta + \mu \\ y(I - \rho W) &= X\beta + \mu \\ y &= (I - \rho W)^{-1} X\beta + (I - \rho W)^{-1} \mu \end{aligned} \quad (7)$$

In matrix form, I represents an $N \times N$ identity matrix in which the diagonal elements equal 1 and the off-diagonal elements are 0. Thus the pre-multiplication of a column vector (i.e., a variable such as y) by I will yield another column vector equal to y. The last line of Equation 7 represents a *spatial lag model* in which the outcome y has been purged of spatial correlation with its neighboring units, except for their influence on the residuals. In fact, this is made clear in the first line of Equation 7 which represents the classic linear regression model in which the exogenous X variables explain the outcome y, net of the influence of the neighboring y.

In the second variation on Equation 4, consider the situation in which $\rho = 0$ and $\lambda \neq 0$. In this scenario, the outcome y is a function a spatial autoregressive processes, without a spatially lagged dependent variable. Equation 4 thus reduces to:

$$y = X\beta + (\lambda W\varepsilon + \mu) \quad (8)$$

Recall that in Equation 3, $\varepsilon = \lambda W\varepsilon + \mu$. Here the error term ε is composed of a spatial autoregressive process $\lambda W\varepsilon$ and an independent, normally distributed, and homoskedastic residual μ. As with Equation 6, endogeneity is present in the equation for ε, as it is determined in part by the neighboring ε. By reworking Equation 8, one can remove the ε from the right side of the equation for the error term:

$$\begin{aligned} \varepsilon &= \lambda W\varepsilon + \mu \\ \varepsilon - \lambda W\varepsilon &= \mu \\ \varepsilon(I - \lambda W) &= \mu \\ \varepsilon &= (I - \lambda W)^{-1} \mu \end{aligned} \quad (9)$$

Substituting the last line of Equation 9 into Equation 8, we obtain:

$$y = X\beta + (I - \lambda W)^{-1}\mu \tag{10}$$

Equation 10 represents a *spatial error model* in which the outcome y is a function of the exogenous X variables, as well as a spatial autoregressive residual. However, in contrast to the original assumption that μ is homoskedastic, μ is now augmented by the spatial disturbance process. The practical result of this is that the error variance will be heteroskedastic when sample units do not have the same number of neighbors (Anselin 2006).[7]

In comparing the spatial lag model in Equation 7 and the spatial error model in Equation 10, it becomes clear that the spatial lag model incorporates aspects of the spatial error model. Specifically, the error terms in both models are assumed to be spatially correlated across units. However, the source of the correlations differs. In the spatial lag model, the residuals are correlated due to the influence of the lagged dependent variable. However, since only one spatial process parameter, ρ, is estimated, it is impossible to disentangle the direct effects of the spatially lagged dependent variable from its indirect effects on the outcome through the error term. Alternatively in the spatial error model, the spatial autoregressive function λ is assumed to be the result of unobserved heterogeneity, usually due to an omitted variable, across the sample units.

Illustration

To illustrate the techniques discussed in this paper, I use homicide data for neighborhoods in the city of St. Louis, Missouri. Neighborhoods are defined here using census tract boundaries from the 2000 census (n = 110).[8] Drawing from the classic Shaw and McKay (1942) model of social disorganization, higher crime rates are expected in neighborhoods characterized by high levels of economic disadvantage, population mobility, and racial and ethnic heterogeneity. Communities exhibiting these characteristics are less likely to be capable of organizing residents to resolve local problems, and instill social control within neighborhood boundaries. It is then the weakening of social controls which in

7. One of the difficulties of estimating spatial dependence models is the inducement of heteroskedasticity. This results as a function of imposing structure on the data through the spatially weighted parameters. It should also be noted that this issue influences not only the spatial error model, but also the spatial lag model. As seen in Equation 5, since the outcome y is estimated as a function of a spatial multiplier process, the error term is also influenced by the same process. Thus, inducing heteroskedasticity in a spatial lag model is possible as well (Anselin 1988).

8. The city of St. Louis had 113 census tracts in the 2000 census. However, three tracts had no population thereby precluding the computation of crime rates, as well as the measurement of structural covariates obtained from census data.

turn allow crime to occur.[9] However as Wilson (1987, 1996) argues, social and economic transformations in large US cities have disproportionately affected predominantly Black neighborhoods by concentrating disadvantage and increasing geographic and social isolation. As a result, racial and ethnic heterogeneity today are often found to be negatively associated with neighborhood crime rates.

The dependent variable is the average homicide rate per 1,000 population over a three-year period from 1999 to 2001. The homicide rates were transformed using the natural log to correct for substantial positive skewness. Since the natural log of zero is undefined, a small constant (.5) was added to the homicide rate for each tract before taking the natural log. The resulting dependent variable ranges in value from –0.69 to 2.16, with a mean of –0.18 and SD of 0.48 (see Table 1 for descriptive statistics).

The data used to measure the independent variables were obtained from the 2000 census. A principal components analysis yielded a three-factor solution, explaining 86.07% of the shared variation in the indicators. The first factor is *Disadvantage*, consisting of (factor loadings in parentheses) percent Black (.700), percent female-headed families with children under 18 (.669), the poverty rate (.808), male joblessness (.777), and average family income (–.886). The second factor is *Instability*, consisting of the percentage of renter-occupied housing units (.974), the percentage of owner-occupied housing units (–.933), and the percentage of housing units that are multi-unit dwellings (.971). The third factor is *Heterogeneity*, consisting of population heterogeneity (.951),[10] and the percentage of the population that is Hispanic (.968). Varimax rotation was used on the final solution to ensure the three independent variables were uncorrelated. All of the independent variables have a mean of 0 and SD of 1.

Table 1 Descriptive statistics (n = 110)

Variable	Mean	SD
Homicide rate	0.47	0.85
Disadvantage	0.00	1.00
Instability	0.00	1.00
Heterogeneity	0.00	1.00

9. The analysis here is intended to demonstrate the use of spatial dependence models, rather than constitute a formal test of social disorganization theory. Considerable research has expanded and elaborated on the original Shaw and McKay (1942) model to include intervening mechanisms such as collective efficacy, and account for spatial processes (see Bursik and Grasmick 1993; Morenoff et al. 2001; Sampson and Groves 1989; Sampson, Raudenbush, and Earls 1997).

10. Heterogeneity is measured as $1-\sum_{i=1}^{5}\left(p_i^2\right)$, where p_i^2 is the squared proportion of the tract population across each of five racial groups: Whites, Blacks, Asian/Pacific Islander, Native American/Aleutian, and Others (Blau 1977; Britt 2000).

Correlations among the variables indicate that disadvantage has a strong and positive correlation with violence ($r = 0.69$, $p < .01$). Additionally, racial heterogeneity has a weak to moderate strength, negative relationship with homicide ($r = -0.28$, $p < .01$). Instability is not significantly correlated with homicide rates across St. Louis neighborhoods ($r = 0.03$, $p > .05$).

I now turn to formally assessing the extent to which spatial autocorrelation exists for homicide. Throughout this example, a first-order queen weights matrix is used.[11] Figure 2 shows a quantile map of the distribution of logged homicide rates across St. Louis census tracts (mean = −0.18). The distribution shows the clustering of high homicide rate communities in the northern half of the city, with a particular concentration on the northeast side. The spatial patterning suggests that positive spatial autocorrelation may be an issue.

Using Moran's *I* as a global measure of spatial autocorrelation, and a first-order queen weights matrix, Figure 3 shows a Moran scatterplot of the spatial lag of logged homicide rates against the logged homicide rates (Anselin 1996). Since Moran's *I* is derived from the mean deviations, it can be interpreted as a coefficient in the regression of *Wy* on *y*. For the logged homicide rates, Moran's $I = 0.4406$ ($p < .01$, using 99 permutations).[12] This leads naturally to the question of whether the internal characteristics of St. Louis neighborhoods generate the observed spatial pattern of homicide rates, or is there some other spatial process associated with homicide itself?

I begin the analysis by estimating an OLS regression of the logged homicide rates on disadvantage. The results in Table 2 show that disadvantage is positively associated with homicide rates. By exponentiating the coefficient, subtracting 1, and multiplying by 100, the coefficient can be transformed into a percentage change in homicide rates associated with a 1 unit change in disadvantage. Specifically, a 1 SD increase in disadvantage is associated with an increase of [exp(0.327) − 1]*100 = 38.7% in the logged homicide rate. As the only explanatory variable in the model, disadvantage explains 47.2% of the variation in neighborhood homicide rates.

The panel at the bottom of Table 2 provides the Moran's test on the OLS residuals, as well as the LM tests for alternative specifications of the spatial model. Moran's *I* for the residuals of the OLS regression is 0.132 ($p = .011$). The results indicate that while controlling for disadvantage has reduced the degree of spatial autocorrelation in homicide rates, significant positive clustering remains. Therefore, we turn to examine the LM tests for alternative specifications. The LM-lag and LM-error tests are both significant, necessitating examination of the robust versions of both tests. The robust LM-lag test statistic is 6.935 ($p < .01$), while the test statistic for the robust LM-error test is 0.411 ($p > .05$).

11. Results were replicated using first-order rook weights, as well as 5-nearest and 10-nearest neighbors. Since the specification of the correct neighbor structure may be debatable, replication of analyses under a variety of weighting structures is strongly suggested.

12. Significance levels for Moran's *I* are based on a permutation process and normal approximation of *I* as a z-score (Anselin et al. 2000; Cliff and Ord 1981).

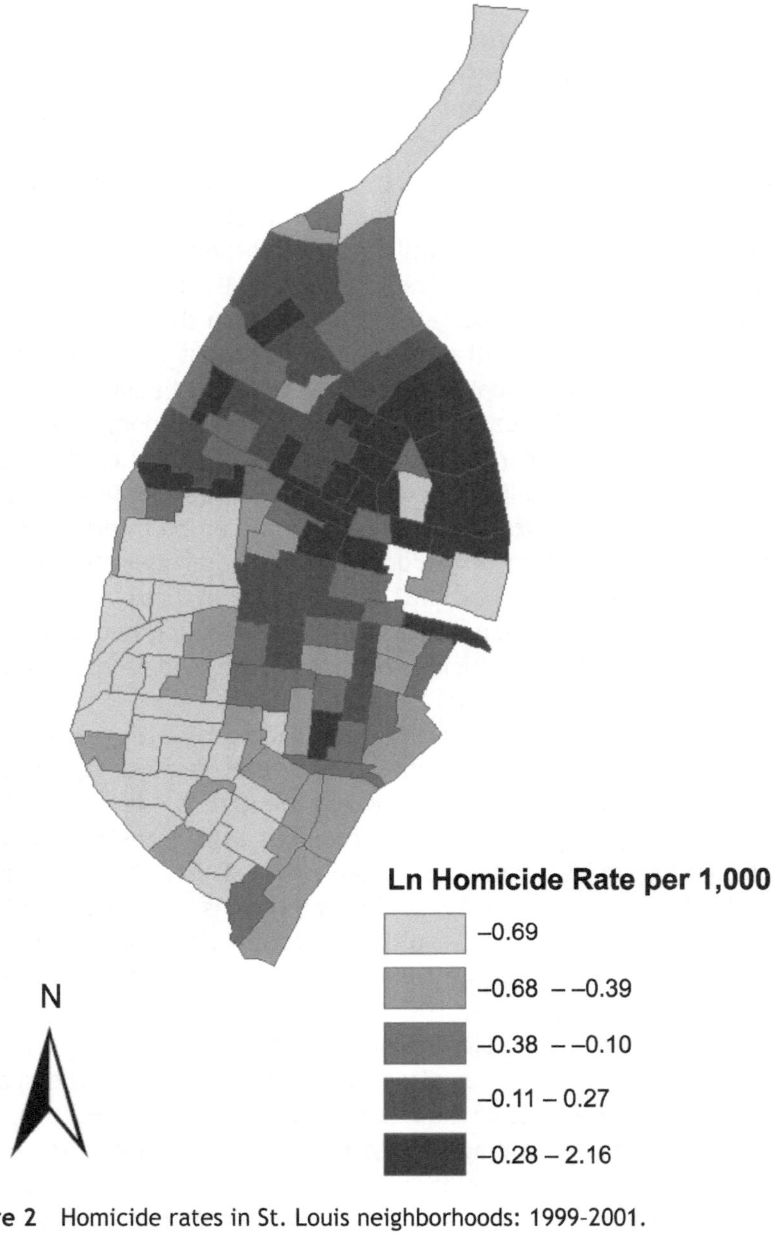

Figure 2 Homicide rates in St. Louis neighborhoods: 1999-2001.

These results indicate that a spatial lag model is preferred over the spatial error model.

Table 3 presents the results from the maximum likelihood spatial lag model, which includes a spatially lagged dependent variable on the right hand side of the equation with ρ representing its coefficient. The results indicate that the spatial lag of the dependent variable is positive and significant ($\rho = .297$, $p < .01$). Therefore, the level of homicide in neighboring j communities has a positive association with homicide rates in neighborhood i, net of the level of disadvantage in

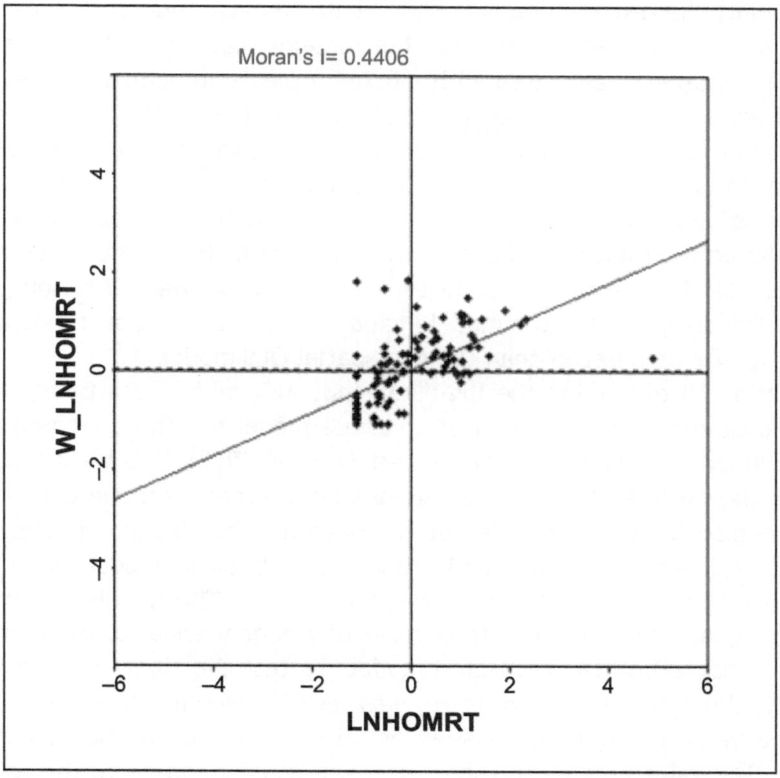

Figure 3 Moran scatterplot of Ln homicide rates.

Table 2 OLS regression of Ln homicide rates on disadvantage (n = 110)

Variable	b	SE
Intercept	−0.178	0.033***
Disadvantage	0.327	−0.033***
R-squared	0.472	
Log-likelihood	−38.580	
F(1, 108)	96.738***	
AIC	81.159	
SC	86.560	
Spatial diagnostics	Value	p
Moran's I (error) = 0.132	2.535	0.0112***
LM lag	11.417	0.0007***
LM error	4.893	0.0270*
Robust LM lag	6.935	0.0085**
Robust LM error	0.411	0.5216

*p < .05; **p < .01; ***p < .001.

i. Additionally the results in Table 3 show that the magnitude of the coefficient for disadvantage has been diminished, but remains significant. An increase of 1 SD in disadvantage is associated with a 0.264 increase in homicide rates across communities. It should be noted here that a comparison of the R-squared value in the spatial lag model is not appropriate here. Since the model is based on maximum likelihood estimation, this is a pseudo-R-squared, and is not comparable to the value given in the OLS results (Anselin 1988). A comparison of model fit statistics across Tables 2 and 3 shows that the log-likelihood increases in Table 3, and both the Akaike Information Criterion (AIC) and Schwarz Criterion (SC) are reduced. This suggests that the model including the spatial lag of the dependent variable fits the data better than the non-spatial OLS model.

In addition to examining the log-likelihood, AIC, and SC statistics, another series of diagnostic test may be used to assess model fit. These include a Wald test, likelihood ratio test, and the LM test (Anselin 1988). The Wald test is the square of the *z*-value of the spatial lag or spatial error coefficient, and uses a chi-square distribution with 1 degree of freedom. The likelihood ratio test is $LR = 2\,|\,L_\theta - L_r\,|$, where L_θ is the log-likelihood of the spatial model, and L_r is the log-likelihood of the restricted or non-spatial model. The likelihood ratio test uses a chi-square distribution with degrees of freedom equal to the number of constrains imposed on the restricted model. To test the fit of a model with a single spatial lag or spatial error term, degrees of freedom will equal 1. The LM test is the value of either the LM-lag or LM-error test performed on the OLS residuals. The values for these three tests will usually adhere to the following inequality: W ≥ LR ≥ LM (Anselin 1988). When this equality is not true, the model should be inspected more carefully for other misspecification problems (e.g., heteroskedasticity, omitted variables, etc.).

In Table 3, the Wald statistic is $(.297/.104)^2 = 2.856^2 = 8.157$. The LR statistics is $[2\,|-34.127 + 38.580\,|] = 8.906$, and the LM-lag test statistic from Table 2 is 11.417. This goes against the conventional order of magnitude for these three

Table 3 Maximum likelihood estimates of spatial lag and spatial error of Ln homicide rates (n = 110)

	Spatial lag		Spatial error	
Variable	*b*	SE	*b*	SE
Intercept	−0.128	0.036***	−0.181	0.045***
Disadvantage	0.264	0.037***	0.296	0.037***
Rho (ρ)	0.297	0.104**		
Lambda (λ)			0.294	0.132*
R-squared	0.522		0.502	
Log-likelihood	−34.127		−36.354	
AIC	74.2535		76.709	
SC	82.3549		82.110	

**p* < .05; ***p* < .01; ****p* < .001.

statistics. Clearly with only disadvantage and the spatially lagged homicide rates included on the right-hand side of the model, omitted variable bias is likely to cause a misspecification error. I will explore this in more detail below.

In this example, the robust LM tests indicated that a spatial lag model was preferred over the spatial error model. However, recall that the spatial lag model incorporates a spatial autoregressive function for the error term. In this way, the spatial lag model encompasses aspects of the spatial error model which does not contain a spatially lagged dependent variable. Therefore, it may be instructive to estimate the spatial error model as a point of comparison. The results of the spatial error model are also presented in Table 3.

The coefficient for the spatial error term, λ, is positive and significant (λ = 0.294, $p < .05$). This estimate is similar to the estimate of ρ for the spatially lagged dependent variable in the spatial lag model. The coefficient estimate for disadvantage is 0.296 ($p < .001$), and the estimated intercept is –0.181 ($p < .001$). These results highlight the similarities that may be obtained in estimating different forms of spatial models. However, the results also show that the log-likelihood for the spatial error model is –36.354, lower than the log-likelihood of the spatial lag model. Additionally, the AIC has increased from 74.254 to 76.709. On the other hand, the SC statistic in the spatial error model is slightly lower than in the spatial lag model at 82.110, suggesting a negligible improvement in model fit. Taken as a whole, the fit statistics indicate that the spatial error model does not fit the data as well as the spatial lag model.

Similar to the diagnostics used with the spatial lag model, we can compare the Wald, LR, and LM statistics for the spatial error model. The Wald statistic is

Table 4 OLS regression of Ln homicide rates on all structural covariates (n = 110)

Variable	*b*	SE
Intercept	–0.178	0.031*
Disadvantage	0.327	0.031*
Instability	0.016	0.031
Heterogeneity	–0.131	0.031*
R-squared	0.550	
Log-likelihood	–29.880	
F(3, 106)	43.127*	
AIC	67.760	
SC	78.562	
Spatial diagnostics	Value	p
Moran's I (error) = –0.009	0.230	0.818
LM lag	1.213	0.271
LM error	0.024	0.876
Robust LM lag	3.777	0.052
Robust LM error	2.588	0.108

*$p < .001$.

$(.294/.132)^2 = 2.227^2 = 4.960$. The LR statistic is $[2|-36.354 + 38.580|] = 4.452$. And the LM-error test statistics from Table 3 is 4.893. As with the spatial lag model, these test statistics do not follow the expected inequality above. Thus there is additional evidence of model misspecification that must be addressed.

At this point, there is evidence of positive spatial autocorrelation among the homicide rates in St. Louis neighborhoods. As expected, the level of neighborhood disadvantage is positively related to violence. Additionally, when the level of disadvantage is controlled, the model residuals exhibit reduced but significant spatial autocorrelation suggesting that a spatial process may be contributing to the generation of homicide rates. The diagnostic results indicate that a spatially lagged dependent variable should be included in the model. However, the resulting maximum likelihood estimates indicate that there is additional model misspecification and that the use of a spatial error model yields similar results.[13] Since only one independent variable was included in the model, it is likely that omitted variable bias may preclude ruling out structural similarity across neighborhoods as the source of misspecification. Therefore, we return to an OLS model in which I include measures of neighborhood instability and racial and ethnic heterogeneity.

Table 4 presents the results from an OLS model in which the dependent variable is the logged homicide rate, and is explained by disadvantage, instability, and heterogeneity. Controlling for these structural characteristics, the average logged homicide rate is −0.178 ($p < .001$). As in Table 2, 1 SD increase in disadvantage is associated with a 38.7% increase in homicide rates. Also as expected, a 1 SD increase in population heterogeneity is associated with a 12.3% decrease in homicide rates. However, residential instability is not significantly associated with homicide in St. Louis neighborhoods.

Importantly, the model fit statistics in Table 4 indicate a substantial improvement over any of the previous specifications. The log-likelihood has increased to −29.880 while the AIC and SC statistics have been reduced to 67.760 and 78.562, respectively. The bottom panel of Table 4 presents the estimate of spatial autocorrelation in the residuals. Moran's $I = -0.009$, and is not significantly different from a spatially random distribution. Thus, including the additional independent variables appears to have explained the spatial distribution of homicide rates across St. Louis neighborhoods.[14] Substantively, neighborhood disadvantage and population heterogeneity are spatially clustered in such a way that the resulting homicide rates have the geographic distribution observed in Figure 2. As an additional check for alternative specifications, the LM-lag statistic is 1.123, while the LM-error statistic is 0.024. Neither of the LM-specification tests is

13. In the OLS regression model, a Breusch-Pagan test for heteroskedasticity yielded a statistic of 26.36 ($p < .001$). However, when the spatial lag of homicide rates was included in the model, the Breusch-Pagan test statistic was 6.47 ($p < .05$). Thus, the inclusion of the spatial lag improved the model specification, but did not eliminate heteroskedasticity in the error term. As discussed above, some heteroskedasticity may be induced by the imposition of a specific spatial structure.

14. The Breusch-Pagan test for the model in Table 4 is 201.75 ($p < .001$), indicating that significant heteroskedasticity remains even with the additional covariates. Additional analyses would be undertaken to identify the source of the mis-specification and estimate a model conforming to the regression assumptions. However, that analysis is beyond the scope of the current paper.

significant, increasing our confidence that the spatial distribution of homicide rates may be explained by structural similarity.

Conclusion

With an increasing focus on community contexts in criminology, researchers are often analyzing data that contain a geographic dimension. As a result, the assumption of independent observations in OLS regression may easily be violated. In such cases, it is reasonable to ask whether or not the observed spatial distributions are generated by the structural similarity of sample units, or by a more complex spatial interaction such as contagion or diffusion. When structural similarity can be ruled out, OLS regression coefficients are likely to be biased and inefficient and models that formally address the spatial processes at work are preferred.

This paper presents a descriptive and illustrative foundation for researchers interested in using spatial dependence models. The basic models shown above may be expanded to address a number of different analytical problems. For example, spatial heterogeneity may occur in the form of structural instability of the regression parameters across geographic space (see Anselin 1988, 1990; Baller et al. 2001). Spatial models have also been adapted for use with panel data techniques (Anselin 1988; Anselin, Le Gallo, and Jayet 2008), and in Bayesian hierarchical and conditionally autoregressive, or CAR, models (Cerda et al. 2009; Jin, Carlin, and Banerjee 2005).

Researchers who are new to spatial data analysis should also be aware that spatial processes are likely to extend beyond the geographic boundary of the sample. For example in this paper, spatial dependence resulting from the influence of neighborhoods surrounding St. Louis city has not been accounted for, and may bias the estimation of spatial dependence effects. This is commonly referred to as the *boundary value problem* or *edge effect* (Anselin 1988). One possible solution to this issue is to estimate a model allowing spatial heterogeneity for units in close proximity to the geographic boundaries. An alternative approach is to drop the boundary units from the sample and re-estimate the model as a robustness check against the full sample.

Finally, while the discussion and example presented here use the concept of space in a geographic sense, this need not be the case. For example, space may take on a social dimension in the form of relational distances along status hierarchies (Black 1997). Mears and Bhati (2006) demonstrate this in their examination of the interaction of resource deprivation and social proximity on homicide in Chicago neighborhoods. Yet, whether space is conceptualized geographically or socially, a developing body of literature in criminology suggests that researchers continue to theorize and assess hypotheses regarding spatial processes. We know that space matters. The failure to assess and account for such processes presents a credible threat to validity for future research using geographically oriented data.

References

Anselin, L. 1988. *Spatial econometrics: Methods and models.* Boston, MA: Kluwer.

Anselin, L. 1990. Spatial dependence and spatial structural instability in applied regression analysis. *Journal of Regional Science* 30: 185-207.

Anselin, L. 1995. Local indicators of spatial autocorrelation—LISA. *Geographical Analysis* 27: 93-115.

Anselin, L. 1996. The Moran scatterplot as an ESDA tool to assess local instability in spatial autocorrelation. In M. Fischer, H. Scholten, and D. Unwin (Eds.), *Spatial analytical perspectives on GIS* (pp. 111-125). London: Taylor & Francis.

Anselin, L. 2006. Spatial econometrics. In T. C. Mills and K. Patterson (Eds.), *Palgrave handbook of econometrics: Vol. 1. Econometric theory* (pp. 901-969). Basingstoke: Palgrave Macmillan.

Anselin, L., and A. Bera. 1998. Spatial dependence in linear regression models with an introduction to spatial econometrics. In A. Ullah and D. E. A. Giles (Eds.), *Handbook of applied econometric statistics* (pp. 237-298). New York: Marcel Drekker.

Anselin, L., A. K. Bera, R. Florax, and M. J. Yoon. 1996. Simple diagnostic tests for spatial dependence. *Regional Science and Urban Economics* 26: 77-104.

Anselin, L., J. Cohen, D. Cook, W. Gorr, and G. Tita. 2000. Spatial analyses of crime. In D. Duffee (Ed.), *Criminal justice: Vol. 4. Measurement and analysis of crime and justice* (pp. 213-262). Washington, DC: National Institute of Justice.

Anselin, L., and R. Florax. 1995. Small sample properties for spatial dependence in regression models: Some further results. In L. Anselin and R. Florax (Eds.), *New directions in spatial econometrics* (pp. 21-74). Berlin: Springer-Verlag.

Anselin, L., J. Le Gallo, and H. Jayet. 2008. Spatial panel econometrics. In L. Matyas and P. Sevestre (Eds.), *The econometrics of panel data: Fundamentals and recent developments in theory and practice* (pp. 625-660). Berlin: Springer-Verlag.

Baller, R. D., L. Anselin, S. F. Messner, G. Deane, and D. F. Hawkins. 2001. Structural covariates of U.S. county homicide rates incorporating spatial effects. *Criminology* 39: 561-590.

Black, D. 1997. *The social structure of right and wrong* (Rev. ed.). New York: Academic Press.

Blau, P. M. 1977. *Inequality and heterogeneity: A primitive theory of social structure.* New York: The Free Press.

Britt, C. L. 2000. Social context and racial disparities in punishment decisions. *Justice Quarterly* 17: 707-732.

Bursik, R. J., and H. G. Grasmick. 1993. *Neighborhoods and crime: The dimensions of effective community control.* New York: Macmillan.

Cerda, M., M. Tracy, S. F. Messner, D. Vlahov, K. Tardiff, and S. Galea. 2009. Misdemeanor policing, physical disorder, and gun-related homicide: A spatial analytic test of "broken windows" theory. *Epidemiology* 20: 533-541.

Cliff, A. D., and J. K. Ord. 1973. *Spatial autocorrelation.* London: Pion.

Cliff, A. D., and J. K. Ord. 1981. *Spatial processes, models, and applications.* London: Pion.

Cohen, J., and G. Tita. 1999. Diffusion in homicide: Exploring a general method for detecting spatial diffusion processes. *Journal of Quantitative Criminology* 15: 451-493.

Cressie, N. 1993. *Statistics for spatial data.* New York: John Wiley & Sons.

Doreian, P. 1980. Linear models with spatially distributed data: Spatial disturbances or spatial effects? *Sociological Methods and Research* 9: 29-60.

Geary, R. C. 1954. The contiguity ratio and statistical mapping. *Incorporated Statistician* 5: 115-145.

Getis, A., and J. K. Ord. 1992. The analysis of spatial association by use of distance statistics. *Geographical Analysis* 24: 198-206.

Griffiths, E., and J. M. Chavez. 2004. Communities, street guns, and homicide trajectories in Chicago, 1980-1995: Merging methods for examining homicide trends across space and time. *Criminology* 42: 941-978.

Jin, X., B. P. Carlin, and S. Banerjee. 2005. Generalized hierarchical multivariate CAR models for areal data. *Biometrics* 61: 950-961.

Kubrin, C. E., and E. A. Stewart. 2006. Predicting who reoffends: The neglected role of neighborhood context in recidivism studies. *Criminology* 44: 165-197.

Mears, D. P., and A. S. Bhati. 2006. No community is an island: The effects of resource deprivation on urban violence in spatially and socially proximate communities. *Criminology* 44: 509-548.

Moran, P. A. P. 1950. Notes on continuous stochastic phenomenon. *Biometrika* 37: 17-23.

Morenoff, J. D., and R. J. Sampson. 1997. Violent crime and the spatial dynamics of neighborhood transition: Chicago 1970-1990. *Social Forces* 76: 31-64.

Morenoff, J. D., R. J. Sampson, and S. W. Raudenbush. 2001. Neighborhood inequality, collective efficacy, and the spatial dynamics of urban violence. *Criminology* 39: 517-560.

Ord, J. K., and A. Getis. 1995. Local spatial autocorrelation statistics: Distributional issues and an application. *Geographical Analysis* 27: 286-306.

Rosenfeld, R., T. M. Bray, and A. Egley. 1999. Facilitating violence: A comparison of gang-motivated, gang-affiliated, and nongang youth homicides. *Journal of Quantitative Criminology* 15: 495-516.

Sampson, R. J., and W. B. Groves. 1989. Community structure and crime: Testing social disorganization theory. *American Journal of Sociology* 94: 774-802.

Sampson, R. J., S. W. Raudenbush, and F. Earls. 1997. Neighborhoods and violent crime: A multilevel study of collective efficacy. *Science* 277: 918-924.

Shaw, C., and H. McKay. 1942. *Juvenile delinquency in urban areas*. Chicago, IL: University of Chicago Press (2nd ed. 1969).

Ward, M. D., and S. K. Gleditsch. 2008. *Spatial regression models*. Thousand Oaks, CA: Sage.

Wilson, W. J. 1987. *The truly disadvantaged: The inner city, the underclass, and public policy*. Chicago, IL: University of Chicago Press.

Wilson, W. J. 1996. *When work disappears: The world of the new urban poor*. New York: Alfred A. Knopf.

Basic Principles and Practices of Structural Equation Modeling in Criminal Justice and Criminology Research

Jacinta M. Gau

Structural equation modeling (SEM) has undergone rapid advances in recent years that have made this technique useful to social scientists studying a variety of topics. The hypothesis-testing and model-evaluation capacity of SEM makes this modeling strategy useful for research in criminal justice and criminology. The flexibility of this strategy and the availability of user-friendly software programs add to the appeal of SEM. This article is a basic introduction to the use of SEM in criminal justice and criminology. An overview of SEM, popular computer programs, and the sequence of steps in building and evaluating models is provided with the intent of offering readers a general roadmap of the use of SEM. The article concludes with a list of recommended readings for those wishing to study this topic in detail.

Introduction

Structural equation modeling (SEM) has become a popular technique within the social sciences. Psychologists, for instance, rely on SEM techniques for scale development. Education specialists use it to track students' academic achievements over time and to evaluate experimental learning interventions. In criminal justice and criminology, SEM is attractive because it offers a flexible array of techniques that can address a variety of research questions and hypotheses. The label "structural equation modeling" is actually an umbrella term that describes a wide spectrum of modeling methodologies. SEM offers options for path models, confirmatory factor analyses, latent growth analyses, multiple-group comparisons, and multilevel modeling.[1] Although it is based on most of

1. It is worth noting that SEM programs are not necessarily the best software for all types of analyses—depending on the nature of the data and the research question under investigation, it may be more appropriate to use other programs that offer similar benefits (e.g., HLM or SAS may be preferable to an SEM program for latent growth or multilevel modeling in some circumstances).

the same assumptions and procedures underlying standard regression, SEM allows the user to do many things that standard regression packages, such as SPSS and SAS, do not.

This article is an introduction to the basics of building SEM models within criminal justice and criminology. The understanding of certain concepts and the knowledge of how to put those concepts into practice are often two different things. This article addresses the latter task of putting knowledge into practice. The reader's competency in the proper use of correlation, regression, and factor analysis is assumed. Readers who need to brush up on these concepts should review a statistics textbook, as these foundations are necessary for understanding and properly using SEM strategies. This article is a general introduction only and will end with a list of suggested readings for those wanting more detail.

What is SEM?

SEM is, as mentioned above, a category of techniques. This type of modeling can be used for factor analytic purposes and for various types of path and structural analyses. The modern generation of SEM software programs boasts user-friendly model-building capabilities that open up SEM to a much wider audience than was reached by the ancestral generation, which was heavy with code and cryptic notation. This is, though, both a benefit and a peril because it is now very easy for people who do not know what they are doing to run SEM models. The new software programs have made it that much more important that researchers fully understand the nature of SEM and follow the requisite procedures for the correct building and testing of models. There are several software programs available, the most popular being LISREL (Jöreskog and Sörbom 2006), Mplus (Muthén and Muthén 2007), EQS (Bentler 2006), and AMOS (Arbuckle 2009). These programs vary in the notation used and the method of code set-up. Users must obtain their program's manual and familiarize themselves with the specifics. Every program is updated periodically, too, so researchers interested in using SEM should be sure they are working with a recent version that will permit them to benefit from the continuous developments that are being made in the statistical science behind this technique.

The statistical foundation of SEM is typically the *variance-covariance matrix* (or co/var matrix). This matrix is, just like it sounds, a matrix of the variances within and the covariances between all the variables in the model. Users can require the program to run off of the correlation matrix instead, but this is discouraged because correlations—unlike covariances—fail to account for variables' standard deviations. Covariances are computed by multiplying the correlation between two variables by each variable's standard deviation (Kline 2005), which means that both correlations and standard deviations are built into covariance estimates. Means are excluded from SEM analyses by default, but many options (e.g., structural regression) permit users to include them when desired. Means analyses are employed when researchers are interested in absolute comparisons and contrasts between groups, such as in pre- and post- or multi-group designs in which the focus is on change over time or differences between groups, respectively.

What SEM does is compare the model that the researcher builds to the observed patterns of covariances within the data. The user specifies a model (discussed below) and the program translates that user-generated model into a series of covariance matrices, which it then compares to the data-generated ones to determine the extent of the match. The basic question is, "How well does the proposed model reproduce the observed patterns in the data?" It is this "theorized-versus-observed" concept that forms the basis for model evaluation and for substantive conclusions stemming from SEM analyses.

Why use SEM?

The first question that a potential SEM user may ask is, Why? What advantages does SEM offer over traditional regression and factor analytic techniques? The answer is that there are multiple advantages. The malleability and wide applicability of SEM permits researchers to go far beyond that to which they are limited by traditional data software such as SPSS or the basic version of SAS. Four general advantages of SEM over other programs can be delineated.

First, SEM offers a more methodologically rigorous way to examine the accuracy and overall quality of models because in addition to factor loadings and regression coefficients, SEM programs produce fit indices (discussed later) that permit the user to evaluate the model in detail. Models can be evaluated on their own merits and/or can be compared to one another in cases in which researchers are interested in the relative quality of competing models. SEM also offers modification indices (also detailed later). If a model does not fit the data well, the program will suggest improvements that would enhance fit. This permits model development and can help the user build successful models. The availability of fit indices enhances the hypothesis-testing capacity of models built in SEM programs, while both fit and modification indices permit much more probing of models and data than traditional software packages allow.

Second, SEM allows factor analysis to be conducted within a confirmatory framework (this is called confirmatory factor analysis or CFA). In CFA, factor structures are hypothesized *a priori* and tested for correctness. This sets SEM apart from programs such as SPSS. The latter offers only relatively superficial reliability statistics such as Cronbach's alpha, which addresses reliability but does not speak to (uni)dimensionality of the underlying construct(s) in question (Cortina 1993; Schmitt 1996). SPSS' factor analysis capacity is limited to exploratory factor analysis, which is data-driven and atheoretical in most applications; furthermore, even in a quasi-confirmatory framework wherein the user forces the data onto a specific number of factors, the evaluation of the model is limited to factor loadings. These exploratory reliability and dimensionality tests are important and useful, but they are cursory and do not suffice for complex questions about factor structures. The fit and modification indices that SEM offers facilitate in-depth assessments of CFA models. SEM packages also make possible several types of CFAs that are not available in any other program. Second-order factors, for instance, can be specified when a researcher suspects that an observed relationship among a group of factors is attributable to the presence of a higher-order factor. This type of modeling is unique to SEM.

A third advantage of SEM over traditional regression (such as ordinary least squares or logistic) is that the former can accommodate multiple dependent and mediating variables. Researchers working with, for instance, ordinary least squares regression are typically limited to a single dependent variable—if they wish to test more than one outcome variable and/or they are interested in indirect effects, they have to run multiple models with various specifications. In SEM, by contrast, all direct and indirect effects of interest can be specified in a single model, and all paths can be tested simultaneously. As in traditional regression analyses, functions are assumed to be linear, but users can specify nonlinear and interactive relationships when necessary. Fit indices are produced for these types of models, as well, and offer the same advantages as those provided in the CFA context—they can be used to evaluate the overall fit and quality of the model, and they can form the basis for comparisons between competing models. SEM, then, gives the user a "big picture" snapshot of the model being examined rather than the relatively piecemeal approach required by regular regression. Total effects can be computed by summing direct and indirect effects, so that the user can identify the magnitude of one variable's impact on another and can determine how much of that total impact is direct and what portion operates indirectly via a third variable. Modification indices are also provided to permit researchers to consider potential improvements in their models.

The fourth reason why SEM is an important modeling tool is that it permits the creation and analysis of *latent variables* (LVs, also referred to as "unobserved variables" and "latent constructs"). LVs are akin to scales that one might create in SPSS by summing highly-correlated items that are thought to tap a single construct. Traditional regression assumes that all variables within a model are measured without error. This is a lofty assumption and one that is not tenable in most cases, but it is especially problematic to the researcher whose primary concern is measurement validity. LVs go beyond simple scales because LVs allow for the assumption of error in the measurement of the observed variables that comprise the construct. In other words, LVs incorporate both observed variables and error terms, whereas scales are made from observed variables only. This makes LVs more realistic than scales. LVs are generally assumed to be continuous, but they can also be specified as categorical when appropriate.

Running a Structural Equation Model

The specific steps that a researcher takes when building, evaluating, and modifying a model depend largely on the question that is under investigation—there is no "One True Recipe" for model construction. There are, however, general guidelines that can be useful to all researchers, regardless of their particular goals. The first step is data cleaning, screening, and exportation. Few SEM programs have data management capabilities, so the data have to be cleaned and formatted in a different software package (e.g., SPSS) and then imported into the SEM program. The second step is model identification, which is where the user ensures that the model has sufficient degrees of freedom. In the third step, the researcher evaluates the model using fit indices. It is standard procedure in SEM-based research to report fit indices and include a discussion of fit. Finally, modification may be required for an ill-fitting model. Should modification be used, an additional step is encouraged: model replication. Each of these steps is detailed below.

Data Screening and Exportation

Like the general linear model under which traditional regression techniques fall, SEM imposes assumptions about the shape and form of data. SEM assumes that variables are distributed normally, that no important variables have been omitted from the model (i.e., that the model is not misspecified), that relationships are linear unless otherwise specified, and that error terms have a mean of zero and are normally distributed, independent, and homoscedastic. There are estimation options that can be used when these assumptions are violated; for instance, latent growth curve modeling adjusts standard errors to accommodate the longitudinal nature of the data. Users considering SEM should be familiar with all the requirements that must be met under the general linear model and should ensure that their data meet those standards. Where special estimation techniques are required, operating manuals should be consulted to ensure that the correct estimation method is selected.

Univariate frequency distributions, descriptive statistics, and histograms should be examined to ensure the absence of extreme skew and kurtosis. When possible, it may is wise to put the model through an ordinary least squares regression analysis to obtain diagnostic statistics for collinearity, autocorrelation, outliers, and other issues that can be problematic. This also provides an opportunity to examine residuals for the presence of harmful non-normality or heteroscedasticity. Only when the researcher is confident that the data pass muster and are ready for analysis should the SEM importation process begin.

SEM programs tend to be pickier about data than standard packages such as SPSS and SAS are. SPSS, for instance, will simply default to listwise deletion to accommodate missing data, but Mplus cannot work with empty cells and requires users to fill them in with values flagged as representing missing data. Most SEM software packages do not have data storage or management capacity, so data preparation has to be done in a different software package and then the file must be imported into the SEM program.[2] There may be a limit to the amount of data that an SEM program can import and restrictions on the file format (some programs can read data directly from SPSS or SAS, whereas others require that the data should be converted to ASCII format). Users should consult their program's manual for the specific steps and rules of the importation process.

The process of importation should begin with the deletion of all variables in the dataset that are not going to be included in the analysis. The variables of interest are the only ones that should be in the data file that is to be imported. The specific order of variables is not important in SEM like it may be in some other types of programs (e.g., HLM for multilevel modeling), but the variable labels do often get deleted during the importation process, so the user must be careful to maintain a record of the order. Once the data have been imported, the user can relabel the variables. It is also worth noting that SEM programs prefer to work with unstandardized variables; importing standardized variables into an SEM package can throw off estimation. It is best to use unstandardized variables whenever possible (Kline 2005). The programs produce standardized path coefficients, so the users are still able to compare the relative strengths of different relationships after the model estimation has taken place.

Model Identification

Model identification is the process of ensuring that the proposed SEM model contains positive degrees of freedom. Models with zero degrees of freedom will run but are useless; models with negative degrees of freedom are also useless and will generally not run. There are two principles to model identification: first, the variances of all LVs must be set, and second, it must be ensured that the number of observed variables exceeds the number of free parameters in the model. Each of these is discussed in turn.

LVs do not have intrinsic variances because they are not measured directly, that is, they are made out of observed variables, but they themselves are unobserved, which means they have no variance. Their variance is set by fixing one of the manifest indicator's loading to 1.0. So, for example, if four indicators are used to construct one LV, then the loading of one of those indicators would need to be set at 1.0 and the other three would be free to vary. Typically, SEM programs will automatically select the first variable in the list of manifest indicators and set that variable's loading at 1.0. The choice of which loading to fix generally will not materially affect the results of the analysis, but if the researcher notices that some of the loadings are very good and others are marginal, then the indicator with the highest loading should be the one selected

2. Mplus, EQS, and AMOS do not have data manipulation or storage capabilities, but LISREL offers PRELIS for this purposes.

to set the variance of the LV because this variable is the best manifest representation of the latent construct.

The second identification issue pertains to the number of estimated or *free* parameters in the model. Most regression-based analyses compute degrees of freedom on the basis of sample size, but SEM computes them according to the number of variables in the analysis and the number of parameters that are to be estimated. Sample size remains an issue in SEM, though; generally, simpler models require sample sizes of no less than 100 and more complex ones require a minimum of 200–300 cases (Kline 2005). The basic idea is that the more complex the model is, the larger the sample size should be. Even though a model with an insufficient sample size might technically be identified, small samples produce unstable and potentially biased parameter estimates and hamper confidence in the results. Users are cautioned, therefore, that even though sample size is not explicitly included in the computation of degrees of freedom, it is still an issue germane to model quality. One should always consider the complexity of the model relative to the size of the sample.

Degrees of freedom in SEM are determined on the basis of what are called *nonredundant elements* in the variance-covariance matrix. The co/var matrix is symmetrical on each side of the diagonal; the nonredundant elements are the covariances on one side of the diagonal and the variances that constitute the diagonal. The formula used to determine the number of nonredundant elements in the co/var matrix for covariance analyses (i.e., SEM models without mean structures) is $v(v + 1)/2$, where v = the number of manifest variables in the analysis. The user must also count the number of free parameters that will be estimated in the model.[3] The number of nonredundant elements in the variance-covariance matrix must be greater than the number of free parameters in the model for the model to be identified (this is called an *overidentified* model). When the two are equal, the model is *just-identified* or *saturated*, and while the analysis will run, there will be no degrees of freedom and the model will therefore be useless. When there are fewer nonredunant elements than free parameters, the model will be *underidentified* (i.e., it will have negative degrees of freedom) and the program will produce an error message.

Ensuring that the number of nonredundant elements in the matrix exceeds the number of free parameters in the model is an important first step for determining identification, but it is not a foolproof method and has particularly pronounced shortcomings with complex models involving, for instance, mean structures or second-order factors. Collinearity can also affect the degrees of freedom during the analysis (Kline 2005), which is a further reason to make sure that diagnostics are conducted before the SEM model is constructed. There is, unfortunately, no guaranteed method for determining that a model is overidentified (Bollen 1989), but there are many ways for a user to tackle the problem to

3. Free parameters include all paths and covariances (except those that are fixed), one variance estimate for each error or disturbance term that accompanies every dependent variable in the analysis (both manifest and latent), a variance estimate for each independent variable, and one path from each error or disturbance term to its corresponding observed or latent variable.

the extent that it can be addressed. Texts such as those of Kline (2005) and Bollen (1989) contain guides for doing one's best to determine identification.

Model Specification and Estimation

The next step is the somewhat self-evident requirement that a model should be created. The user must instruct the program as to the variables that will be used and the relationships that are to be tested. This is done in what is called an input file. Words like "on" and "with" represent regressions and covariances, respectively. Symbols such as "=" and "+" permit the user to construct regression equations such as $y = bx + e$ using the variable names and, if applicable, error notations. Programs differ with respect to syntax and symbols, so researchers must familiarize themselves with the language that their program utilizes before constructing the input file.

Programs typically assume that parameters such as the "*b*" coefficient in $y = bx + e$ are free to vary, and that the user wishes them to be estimated; however, there are instances when researchers wish to fix these parameters so that they are constrained to be equal to a specified value. This is done when, for instance, a researcher wishes to fix the variance of a latent variable using that of a manifest indicator by constraining the coefficient to 1.0 in the input file (this would make the equation $y = 1.0x + e$). In the context of invariance testing, the researcher may wish to fix the value of the coefficient to some other number as indicated by prior theory and empirical analyses. Any number can be used, so long as the choice is rational and justified.

Before the model is run, the user must select an estimation method. The default method in SEM is maximum likelihood (ML), and most programs contain many variations of ML estimation to accommodate the specific characteristics of a dataset. EQS, for instance, has a robust ML option available for data that are somewhat skewed. Mplus offers ML estimation for nested sampling designs. There are also options for weighted, unweighted, and generalized least squares. Each program's manual lists the estimation methods offered by that program. The estimation method that a user selects depends on the user's knowledge of the data collection method, the variables' levels of measurement, and the distributions.

Another thing to consider at this stage is whether any of the dependent variables in the analysis are categorical. SEM assumes that all dependent variables are continuous, so if a dependent variable is categorical and not specified as such, the output will be erroneous and the results will be uninterpretable. User manuals contain directions for specifying outcome variables as categorical.

Model Evaluation

As described above, building SEM models involves (indirectly) constructing covariance matrices. The program then compares the built matrices to the actual patterns of covariances within the dataset. Structural equation models are evaluated according to the "fit" between the observed covariance matrices and the ones posited by the researcher. The criteria used to judge this fit are called, not surprisingly, *fit indices*. There are several types of fit indices, and there has been extensive debate among SEM experts as to which ones are the best. This dispute has prompted a consensus that it is always prudent to report multiple indices (see Hu and Bentler 1999), so that any given index's shortcomings can be compensated for by another one's strengths. It is important to note that some indices can be used only with certain types of model estimation strategies; in other words, a given index that is available with, for example, ML estimation may not be available for robust ML or for generalized least squares. Different software programs also offer different indices. The choice of indices, then, may be at least partially driven by the estimation method employed and/or the program used.

One index that is customarily reported is the model's chi-square (χ^2) value. This index is called the *chi-square goodness-of-fit test*, but it is actually a *badness*-of-fit measure because a significant chi-square value means that there is a significant difference between the theorized and the observed covariance matrices. As it is generally the goal of the SEM user to specify a model that adequately reproduces the data, a significant chi-square is worrisome. This index comes with two important caveats, though. First, the index is distributed as a χ^2 only asymptotically; therefore, the shape of the distribution is unknown in small samples, and as a result, statistical significance can be difficult to determine (Hu and Bentler 1995). Second, SEM usually requires large sample sizes, but large samples cause the chi-square value to nearly always be statistically significant. As both small and large sample sizes cause statistical problems with χ^2, this index is of limited practical use. It should not be given much weight. Despite this problem, though, most people who use SEM in the criminal justice/criminology context report this statistic.

One thing that the χ^2 index is useful for is in comparing nested models to determine whether a trimmed model offers a statistically significant improvement in fit over its more complex counterpart. A fundamental goal in SEM is to produce the best model that contains the fewest possible parameters. Researchers are sometimes interested, then, in comparing a full model with a parsed model. A three-factor model might, for instance, be compared to a two-factor model to determine whether three factors truly are necessary or whether two suffice. The two-factor model (the simpler one) would be nested within the three-factor model (the more complex one). Another example would be comparing a model that tests for indirect effects (the more complex model) to the one that contains direct effects only (the nested model). Comparing full to restricted models should only be done, of course, on the basis of theory and logic. The researcher should have an articulable, *a priori* rationale for constructing the parsed model from the full one and testing the two against one another. The *chi-square difference statistic* (χ^2_D) is computed by calculating the difference between the two chi-square values. The resulting χ^2_D value is distributed along the chi-square distribution and has degrees of freedom (df_D) equal to the difference between the degrees of freedom for the respective models.[4] Each deletion of a single path produces an increase of one degree of freedom. The null hypothesis in this test is that there is no difference between how well the two models represent the data. A nonsignificant χ^2_D statistic means that the null is not rejected or, in other words, the two models perform equally well. In this case, the parsed model is probably the one that should be accepted because simpler models are preferable to more complex ones when both evince good fit. A statistically significant χ^2_D, on the other hand, means that the null hypothesis of equal fit must be rejected and the parsed model is no good, that is, removing one or more parameters cased a statistically significant increase in the chi-square model and resulted in worse fit relative to the full model (see Kline 2005; see also Bentler and Bonett 1980 for a more technical rendition). Like its χ^2 analogue, χ^2_D is sensitive to sample size, and large samples can cause spurious statistical significance of the χ^2_D statistic (Marsh and Hau 1996). This test is available for nested models only and cannot be used to compare two entirely different models.

A panoply of *supplementary fit indices* has been proposed by SEM experts in an attempt to address the shortcomings of the χ^2 statistic. These indices are of two types: absolute and incremental. The basic differentiating feature is the precise way in which each type evaluates fit (for details, see Bentler and Bonett 1980; Bollen 1989; and Hu and Bentler 1995, 1998, 1999). In criminal justice and criminological studies, the distinction is typically not addressed. What matters in practical applications of SEM are the *cutoff criteria* (i.e., minimum and maximum thresholds) that have been established by SEM experts to serve as guidelines for determining when an index implies an acceptable fit and when it indicates a poor one. With one exception (the root mean square error of approximation [RMSEA], as discussed below), supplementary fit indices do not have known sampling distributions and inferential tests for statistical significance are thus precluded. It is important to avoid adopting too rigid an approach to fit index examination—models should not be judged in a simple "accept-or-reject" dichotomous fashion but should, rather, be assessed holistically using multiple fit indices, factor loadings and regression coefficients, and the researcher's knowledge of and good judgment about the theory being tested.

There are two crucial considerations to keep in mind during the ensuing discussion of fit indices. The first is that any given model's good fit is not evidence that this is the only or even the best model that could be created to represent the observed patterns in the data. Good fit merely means that this particular model does an adequate job explaining these patterns—it does not rule out the existence of alternative specifications that would yield equal or

4. Researchers who wish to drop more than one path from the full model to create the restricted model can do so, either one path at a time or all paths at once. Dropping multiple paths simultaneously, however, lends uncertainty to the interpretation of χ^2_D if it emerges as statistically significant because there is no way to tell which of the dropped paths produced a meaningful reduction in fit. Dropping paths one by one solves this problem because the changes can be evaluated individually.

even better fit. Whenever possible, competing models should be tested so that the researcher can compare relative fit and make a judgment about which model appears superior to the other. The researcher might find that although one model fits the data adequately, the other one fits extremely well, and had the second one not been analyzed, the first one may have been fallaciously accepted. Things that can be done to test competing models include, but are not limited to: (1) dropping select paths to determine the strength and importance of a given relationship between two or more variables; (2) specifying different numbers of factors, such as testing a two-factor model against a one-factor version or comparing a first-order CFA to a second-order model; and (3) altering the direction of a path where there is a question of endogeneity or nonrecursivity between two variables. Whenever possible, a minimum of two models should be specified for purposes of comparing fit and helping to ensure that the model ultimately decided upon is truly the best one.

The second consideration critical to fit indices and model evaluation is parsimony. SEM's capacity for highly complex regression systems raises a temptation to build dense, cobweb-like models with multiple paths going in all directions. Complex models, though, are problematic and ill-advised for two reasons. The first is that models with a multitude of free parameters may be saturated or even underidentified. As described above in the section on model identification, just-identified models' fit cannot be evaluated at all (it will always be perfect because there are no degrees of freedom) and underidentified models will not run. The second reason that parsimony is favored is that free parameters have a tendency to artificially inflate fit indices even when the model is overidentified. Opting against insertion of a path between two variables is tantamount to constraining the coefficient of that path to zero. Fixing paths' values imposes restrictions on models. Removing these restrictions reduces the methodological demands upon the models and allows the data to drive the fit indices upward irrespective of the theoretical soundness of certain parameters' freedom. All else being equal, simpler models are preferable to complex ones despite the fact that the former may yield lower fit indices than the latter (Mulaik et al. 1989). Fit indices, then, should always be interpreted through a lens of model complexity, and paths should never be added simply because they improve the fit of the model. With these considerations in mind, the discussion now turns to the different supplementary fit indices.

One commonly reported supplementary measure is the *comparative fit index* (CFI; Bentler 1990). This is an incremental index and is bounded at 0.0 and 1.0. The closer to 1.0 the CFI statistic is, the better the model fits the data. Values of 0.95 and above are indicative of very good fit (Hu and Bentler 1999), but a model should be considered potentially useful anytime the CFI is at least 0.90 (see Cheung and Rensvold 2002). The 0.95 minimum may be too stringent. This underscores the importance of a multiple-index strategy: when a CFI is above 0.90 but below 0.95, other indices can help the researcher determine the overall quality of the model. If the CFI is 0.90 and the other measures indicate good fit, then the model may have merit; on the other hand, if the CFI is 0.90 and the other measures are outside their ranges for acceptable fit, then the model should be considered poor. When the CFI is at least 0.95, it would be expected that the other indices would also evidence good fit.

Two other statistics are Jöreskog and Sörbom's (1984) goodness-of-fit index (GFI) and its counterpart, the adjusted goodness-of-fit index (AGFI). Both are absolute measures and range from 0.0 to 1.0, with values of 0.90 and above indicative of good fit (Marsh and Hau 1996). The difference between the two is that the AGFI includes a penalty for overparameterization; that is, the addition of parameters will cause a drop in the AGFI because, as aforementioned, SEM theory embodies a predilection for models that are as parsimonious as possible. Adding parameters on an *a posteriori* basis can cause an artificial inflation in fit due to chance variations in a particular sample that are meaningless—or at least unfounded—from a theoretical standpoint. The AGFI rewards models that have high degrees of freedom and penalizes those with low degrees of freedom. Although the GFI and AGFI models are fairly widely used in criminal justice and criminological research, some SEM experts have expressed doubt about their accuracy and usefulness (Hu and Bentler 1998; see also Fan, Thompson, and Wang 1999).

The RMSEA (see Hu and Bentler 1998) and the standardized root mean squared residual (SRMR; Jöreskog and Sörbom 1981) are indicators of error between the hypothesized model and the true covariance matrix underlying the data. Both are absolute measures. The RMSEA penalizes model complexity, but the SRMR does not (Marsh and Hau 1996). Neither measure has a specific range in the same sense that the CFI, GFI, and AGFI do—their lowest value is 0.0, and they increase as the discrepancy between the hypothesized and true models worsens. The goal with these two, then, is for them to be as close to zero as possible. Generally, values less than or equal to 0.05 are desirable (Marsh and Hau 1996), but this criterion is somewhat draconian and can lead to the erroneous rejection of models if followed unyieldingly (Hu and Bentler 1999). A better guideline is that RMSEA values between 0.10 and 0.06 are acceptable, while values of 0.05 and below are very good. The SRMR is sensitive to model misspecification and tends to be robust across different sample sizes and estimation techniques, which makes it a desirable and useful statistic (Hu and Bentler 1998). SRMR values above 0.06 generally imply questionable fit, though values of up to 0.11 may be tolerable if concomitant indices are within their respective acceptable ranges (Hu and Bentler 1999).

Another measure that has been proposed is the Critical N (CN; Hoelter 1983). The CN is the maximum sample size at which the null hypothesis of adequate fit would not be rejected. Values equal to or greater than 200 are considered good. Hu and Bentler (1998) found that the CN was not sufficiently sensitive to model misspecification to render it a beneficial index and they discouraged its use.

The final index that will be discussed here is the chi-square/degrees of freedom ratio, which researchers can compute by hand. The smaller the ratio, the better the fit. Wheaton, Muthén, Alwin, and Summers (1977) suggested that ratios of 5.0 and lower are best; however, the choice of 5.0 as the maximum value was somewhat arbitrary. This index has not been included in the rigorous simulation studies that have been conducted to examine the quality of other indices, so its accuracy and empirically justified maximum value are not known. Researchers who choose to use it look for values as close to 1.0 as possible (e.g., Smith and Patterson 1985).

The above is not an exhaustive list of fit indices; quite to the contrary, many measures have been proposed throughout the years. Many of the oldest ones have been modified, discredited, or supplanted by more statistically sophisticated versions. Readers interested in more information about the myriad of indicators that have been—and to some extent, are still being—used are referred to Bentler and Bonett (1980), Bollen (1989), Fan et al. (1999), and Hu and Bentler (1999).

Model Modification

One of the biggest advantages of SEM over traditional regression techniques is the ability to evaluate the overall fit of the model. Many models, though, do not fit well on the initial specification. This is sometimes the result of the model simply being misspecified; that is, the model may be fatally flawed. Other times, poor fit might result from something minor, such as two factor indicators being highly correlated. It would be hasty and premature to simply throw out a model that appears to be a poor fit to the data. When fit indices demonstrate that a model is not very good, researchers turn to *modification indices* to determine the ways in which the model might be improved to produce an acceptable fit.

Modification indices are usually contained in the last portion of the SEM program output. They are listed in the order from the modifications that would cause the greatest increases in fit to the ones that would produce the smallest increases. Fit improvement is judged by a chi-square difference test wherein the program compares the chi-square measure of fit for the current model to the chi-square fit index of a hypothetical model with the proposed modification made. These suggested changes provide the user with a range of options for improving the model.

Model modification indices are useful and always worth looking at, but they can also be dangerous because they tempt users to alter models based on data rather than on theory. Model modification should never be done unless there is defensible justification for the changes that are made. This justification can be based on theory or prior studies' empirical findings or it can be based on logic and reasoned judgment. If, for instance, a modification index suggests an alteration in the model that is consistent with the way in which prior researchers have conceptualized the relationship between the variables at issue, then the researcher might be wholly justified in making this change. When a researcher is testing a full model against a restricted version and the modification indices show that inserting the omitted path(s) into the parsed model would substantially improve fit, this can be taken as evidence that the full model is the better one.

One change that is commonly suggested by modification indices is to permit two or more manifest indicators to covary (or, more specifically, to permit their error terms to covary; SEM permits that only their error terms can be linked). The different indicators of a single factor will typically be correlated with each other at least modestly; after all, they are all supposed to be tapping a single underlying construct. Sometimes, though, the correlation is so high that failing to specify a covariance between them causes a form of model misspecification. One typical reason for this is content overlap, in which two indicators are worded similarly or are otherwise conceptually redundant with one another. It may be permissible to free the parameter between these two variables' error terms.

Any time a model is modified in a substantial way, replication is strongly encouraged. Modification, even when it comports with theory and/or prior literature, is inherently a *post hoc* procedure—it is data-driven and can look suspiciously like "mining" or "fishing." Chance variations in particular samples, moreover, can result in erroneous conclusions if the researcher mistakenly interprets sampling error-based idiosyncrasies as substantively meaningful. To prevent capitalizing on chance variations in the data and to assuage concerns that a modified model's good fit is the result of impermissible *post hoc* examination, a researcher who modifies a model should subject the modified version to testing with a new sample. The most methodologically rigorous way to do this is to gather a new sample and test the modified model on the new data. This is rarely feasible for researchers in criminology and criminal justice, so another option is to randomly divide the original sample into halves and use the first half for model development and the second half for model replication. (This can be done only when the sample size is large enough so that even when split in half, there are enough cases in each subsample to permit confidence in the parameter estimates.) A model that is modified and then re-tested on a new sample is more reliable than a model that is simply tweaked in such a way as to make it fit.

Conclusion

SEM offers numerous benefits over traditional regression-based analyses. It makes possible several modeling strategies that are not available under other statistical modeling frameworks and it facilitates rigorous evaluation of a hypothesized model's fit to the data that the model allegedly represents. Advances in software and computer technology have made SEM accessible and user-friendly to researchers who are knowledgeable about quantitative methods but who do not have extensive training in matrix algebra or computer code-writing. Greater accessibility, though, makes prudence and responsibility paramount: as authors of studies, criminal justice and criminology researchers must exercise caution and good judgment; as peer-reviewers of others' work, they must be vigilant for mistakes that undermine the accuracy of both the analysis and the conclusions drawn therefrom. SEM is becoming an ever more sophisticated and potential-laden endeavor. It has been and will continue to be a valuable contribution to the scientific advancement of criminal justice and criminology.

References

Arbuckle, J. L. 2009. *AMOS*. Chicago, IL: SPSS.

Bentler, P. M. 1990. Comparative fit indexes in structural models. *Psychological Bulletin* 107 (2): 238-246.

Bentler, P. M. 2006. *EQS 6.1 structural equations program*. Encino, CA: Multivariate Software.

Bentler, P. M., and D. G. Bonett. 1980. Significance tests and goodness of fit in the analysis of covariance structures. *Psychological Bulletin* 88 (3): 588-606.

Bollen, K. A. 1989. *Structural equations with latent variables*. New York, NY: John Wiley.

Cheung, G. W., and R. B. Rensvold. 2002. Evaluating goodness-of-fit indexes for testing measurement invariance. *Structural Equation Modeling* 9 (2): 233-255.

Cortina, J. M. 1993. What is coefficient alpha? An examination of theory and applications. *Journal of Applied Psychology* 78 (1): 98-104.

Fan, X., B. Thompson, and L. Wang. 1999. Effects of sample size, estimation methods, and model specification on structural equation modeling fit indexes. *Structural Equation Modeling* 6 (1): 56-83.

Hoelter, J. W. 1983. The analysis of covariance structures: Goodness-of-fit indices. *Sociological Methods and Research* 11 (3): 325-344.

Hu, L., and P. M. Bentler. 1995. Evaluating model fit. In R. H. Hoyle (Ed.), *Structural equation modeling: Concepts, issues, and applications* (pp. 76-99). Thousand Oaks, CA: SAGE Publications.

Hu, L., and P. M. Bentler. 1998. Fit indices in covariance structure modeling: Sensitivity to underparamterized model misspecification. *Psychological Methods* 3 (4): 424-453.

Hu, L., and P. M. Bentler. 1999. Cutoff criteria for fit indexes in covariance structure analysis: Conventional criteria versus new alternatives. *Structural Equation Modeling* 6 (1): 1-55.

Jöreskog, K. G., and D. Sörbom. 1981. *LISREL V: Analysis of linear structural relationships by the method of maximum likelihood*. Chicago, IL: National Educational Resources.

Jöreskog, K. G., and D. Sörbom. 1984. *LISREL VI user's guide* (3rd ed.). Mooresville, IN: Scientific Software.

Jöreskog, K. G., and D. Sörbom. 2006. *LISREL 8.8 for Windows* [Computer software]. Lincolnwood, IL: Scientific Software International.

Marsh, H. W., and K. Hau. 1996. Assessing goodness of fit: Is parsimony always desirable? *Journal of Experimental Education* 64 (4): 364-391.

Mulaik, S. A., L. R. James, J. Van Alstine, N. Bennett., S. Lind, and C. D. Stilwell. 1989. Evaluation of goodness-of-fit indices for structural equation models. *Psychological Bulletin* 105 (3): 430-445.

Muthén, B. O., and L. K. Muthén. 2007. *Mplus*. Los Angeles, CA: Muthén & Muthén.

Schmitt, N. 1996. Uses and abuses of coefficient alpha. *Psychological Assessment* 8 (4): 350-353.

Smith, D. A., and E. B. Patterson. 1985. Latent-variable models in criminological research: Applications and a generalization of Joreskog's LISREL model. *Journal of Quantitative Criminology* 1 (2): 127-158.

Wheaton, B., B. Muthén, D. F. Alwin, and G. F. Summers. 1977. Assessing reliability and stability in panel models. *Sociological Methodology* 8: 84-136.

Recommended Readings for General Information about SEM

Byrne, B. M. 2006. *Structural equation modeling with EQS: Basic concepts, applications, and programming* lpar;2nd ed.). Mahwah, NJ: Lawrence Erlbaum.

Hoyle, R. H. 1995. *Structural equation modeling: Concepts, issues, and applications.* Thousand Oaks, CA: SAGE Publications.

Kline, R. B. 2005. *Principles and practice of structural equation modeling* (2nd ed.). New York, NY: The Guilford Press.

Recommended Readings for example SEM Applications to Criminal Justice and Criminology

Gau, J. M., and T. C. Pratt. 2008. Broken windows or window dressing? Citizens' (in)ability to tell the difference between disorder and crime. *Criminology & Public Policy* 7 (2): 163-194.

Piquero, A. 1999. The validity of incivility measures in public housing. *Justice Quarterly* 16 (4): 793-818.

Worrall, J. L. 2006. The discriminant validity of perceptual incivility measures. *Justice Quarterly* 23 (3): 360-383.

Meta-Analysis in Criminal Justice and Criminology: What It is, When It's Useful, and What to Watch Out for

Travis C. Pratt

Meta-analyses are becoming more common in the criminal justice and criminological literature. While much of the published work related to the technique is focused on the more technical aspects of the statistical methods that have been developed for meta-analysis, less common are broader—and perhaps more critical—discussions concerning various issues associated with the method. Accordingly, this article presents an overview of meta-analysis in the context of what have become three of the more important issues within the meta-analysis literature in recent years: (1) the conditions under which meta-analyses are, and are not, most useful, (2) the dilemma of whether or not to include unpublished work in the sample of studies to be analyzed, and (3) the choice of bivariate versus multivariate effect size estimates to be synthesized. The objective is to take these issues out of what has arguably been debates about technical orthodoxy and instead to place them into a broader research context within criminal justice and criminology.

Introduction

Meta-analyses are becoming more and more common in the criminal justice and criminological literature. While the technique emerged initially within the field in the area of correctional treatment and predictors of recidivism (Andrews et al. 1990; Bonta, Law, and Hanson 1998; Gendreau, Little, and Goggin 1996; Izzo and Ross 1990; Lipsey 1992; Lipsey and Wilson 1993; Loeber and Stouthamer-Loeber 1986), it has also been used to assess the state of the literature with regard to criminal justice systems dynamics (Daly and Bordt 1995; Franklin, Franklin, and Pratt 2006; Makarios and Pratt, in press; Pratt 1998; Pratt and Maahs 1999; Whatley 1996) and to establish the empirical status of criminological theories (Paternoster 1987; Pratt and Cullen 2000, 2005; Pratt, Cullen, Blevins, Daigle, and Madensen 2006; Pratt et al., in press; see also Hubbard and

Pratt 2002; Pratt, Cullen, Blevins, Daigle, and Unnever 2002; Pratt, McGloin, and Fearn 2006; Walters 1992).

The problem is that much of the published work related to the technique is focused on the more technical aspects of the statistical methods that have been developed for meta-analysis (Hedges and Olkin 1985; Lipsey and Wilson 2001; Raudenbush, Becker, and Kalaian 1988; Raudenbush and Bryk 2002). These works are enormously useful for scholars as they prepare to conduct a meta-analysis and they should be mandatory reading for anyone considering using the technique. Even so, less common are broader—and perhaps more critical—discussions concerning various issues associated with the method (for exceptions, see Lipsey 2003; Pratt 2002; Shaffer and Pratt 2009). There is a risk, therefore, if we get too hyper-focused on the technical nuances of this method that larger considerations may end up getting lost—particularly with regard to those issues most relevant for crime and justice scholars faced with the task of systematically organizing the body of research in a given area.

Accordingly, the purpose of the present work is not to replace these primary sources, but rather to augment them with a more general discussion of the key issues facing meta-analysts in contemporary criminological research. To that end, following an overview of meta-analysis itself, this article critically discusses what have become three of the more important issues within the meta-analysis literature in recent years: (1) the conditions under which meta-analyses are, and are not, most useful, (2) the dilemma of whether or not to include unpublished work in the sample of studies to be analyzed, and (3) the choice of bivariate versus multivariate effect size estimates to be synthesized. The objective here is not to provide the definitive word on these issues, but rather to take them out of what has arguably been debates about technical orthodoxy and instead to place them into a broader context so that scholars may understand more clearly when a meta-analysis will live up to its promise of organizing criminological knowledge in a way that will benefit the field.

Meta-Analysis and the Systematic Organization of Knowledge

The empirical status of the research on any particular topic in criminal justice or criminology is usually established via the traditional narrative review of the research literature. In this method, studies are described discursively and afforded relative importance according to the reviewer. At a most basic level, this approach may involve "vote counting," in which the number of studies showing a statistically significant relationship between the variables of interest are tallied up versus those that do not find such a relationship (e.g., the number of studies showing or not showing that a treatment intervention "works" to reduce recidivism). If more studies are statistically significant than are not, then the reviewer typically concludes that, on balance, the research literature indicates that a relationship exists.

These reviews can be enormously useful since, if focused on the details of the studies, they may yield special insights and illuminate new pathways for future research. Such narrative reviews do, however, have three potential limitations. First, they are qualitative and thus depend on the judgment of their authors to tell the reader what the research shows. As qualitative assessments, however, even the most carefully conducted narrative reviews often provide only crude estimates of the degree to which certain key variables are related (see, e.g., Burton and Cullen 1992; Kempf 1993). Second, when the research findings are mixed—with some studies finding significant results while others do not—there can be a legitimate dispute over what the body of research "really says." In such cases, a range of biases may creep into the discussion and influence the lens through which the body of research is perceived (for an example in the area of rehabilitation, see Cullen and Gendreau 2000). Indeed, conflicting interpretations of the existing empirical evidence on a given research question are not uncommon, and even consistent interpretations could conceivably be attributable to similar biases and misreadings of the literature (Glass 1977; Light and Smith 1971; Pillemer and Light 1980). Finally, the variability in study outcomes makes it difficult to falsify a given thesis or theory. Thus, there is the potential for ideas to linger on longer than they should not because they have scientific merit, but rather because the imprecise way in which knowledge is organized in a narrative review leaves the door open for bad ideas to still claim empirical legitimacy if studies supporting their such ideas can still be located.

As an alternative to the traditional narrative review, meta-analysis entails "the application of statistical procedures to collections of empirical findings for the purpose of integrating, synthesizing, and making sense of them" (Niemi 1986, p. 5). Meta-analysis attempts to integrate the findings of multiple independent tests of a similar hypothesis in a more objective manner by treating the empirical study as the unit of analysis. Researchers may then draw inferences based on the effect size (or predictive capacity) of relationships between variables (Cohen 1977; Hunter, Schmidt, and Jackson 1982). As Pratt and Cullen (2005) pointed out, another way of thinking about a meta-analysis is to consider the computation of a batting average in baseball. In some games, a player may go without a hit; in other games, he (or she) may get multiple base hits; and, in some games, a player may have two or three at-bats and in other games four or five at-bats. To calculate a batting average, one does not simply count how many games in which a player was able to get a base hit (this would be analogous to the vote counting method mentioned above). Instead, a batting average is computed by summing the average batting average per game weighted by the number of at-bats per game. In a like way, in a meta-analysis, each study can be treated like an individual game: the degree of relationship between an independent and dependent variable is like the batting average for a player in a given game. The overall batting average—or effect size—is how well the independent variable "hits" or is related to the dependent variable across all "games" or studies.

In addition, it is possible in batting averages to calculate a player's batting average under a variety of conditions, such as whether the pitcher was lefthanded or righthanded, whether or not there were runners in scoring position, whether the game was played in certain stadiums (such in Coors Field and the light air of Denver or in the short fences of Boston's Fenway Park), and so on. Similarly, in a meta-analysis, it is possible to examine whether an array of methodological factors may condition the effect size of the relationships between the independent to the dependent variables. Thus, separate effect sizes can be calculated when a study is longitudinal, when known predictors of the dependent variable are or are not controlled, when a certain measure of a variable is used, or when a certain unit of analysis is used, and so on. In each case, it is thus possible to examine statistically how an effect size will increase or decrease across such methodological variations.

Advantages of Meta-Analysis

Despite this expansion in its application and the growing roster of researchers employing the technique, some lingering doubts remain about the utility and validity of meta-analysis in criminal justice and criminology. To be sure, methodological inconsistencies have yielded independent meta-analyses of the same set of literature that reach radically different conclusions—especially when such disagreements center around how diligent researchers should be in exploring the degree to which the effect sizes vary across different methodological specifications (e.g., whether separate effect sizes should be calculated by different types of intervention and across different samples of individuals, see Andrews et al. 1990; Lab and Whitehead 1990; Whitehead and Lab 1989).[1] The primary result of such discrepancies has been the charge that many meta-analyses are methodologically soft (Logan and Gaes 1993). Even so, meta-analyses are gaining in popularity among researchers and policy makers largely due to their parsimonious format: a large body of literature can be summarized in relative short order (Hunter and Schmidt 1996). Furthermore, scholars have noted four distinct advantages of meta-analysis over traditional narrative reviews of literature.

First, meta-analysis generally provides a single, precise estimate of the magnitude (or effect size) of a specified empirical relationship between two variables. In contrast, and as stated above, narrative reviews of literature, at best, may employ a form of vote counting. A key advantage of meta-analytic reviews of research literature therefore is that they may go beyond the simple significant-non-significant dichotomy to enable comparisons of the relative *strength* of key theoretical relationships. Second, meta-analysis is also capable

1. The mean treatment effect size estimates for the Whitehead and Lab (1989) and Andrews et al. (1990) studies were similar—both revealed a treatment effect of approximately .20. Their disagreement centered primarily around the substantive interpretation of a treatment effect of that size (i.e., whether a 20% reduction in recidivism is "good enough").

of yielding the effect size of empirical relationships under different methodological conditions. For example, there are certain controversies surrounding the empirical validity of a link between unemployment and crime at the aggregate level (e.g., see Piehl 1998; Pratt and Lowenkamp 2002). In particular, questions have been raised concerning how the unemployment-crime (U-C) relationship varies across units of analysis (e.g., cities versus states), for different types of crimes (e.g., violent versus property crimes), and across different types of research designs (e.g., cross-sectional versus longitudinal designs). Narrative reviews of the U-C literature (e.g., see Chiricos 1987) have highlighted trends in how such methodological variations may influence the U-C relationship, such as how the effect of unemployment rates on crime rates appears to be stronger at the city level, for property crimes, and in cross-sectional research designs. Yet a meta-analysis of the same body of literature by Pratt and Cullen (2005) went go beyond such clinical eyeballing, and was instead able to assess whether these apparent differences were statistically significant, and provided precise estimates of *how much* the U-C relationship varied according to methodological differences across empirical studies.

Third, as with other quantitative studies, the methodological decisions used in a meta-analysis can be made public. In short, how studies are coded and categorized may be listed and described in the same manner as the empirical studies being reviewed. This element of meta-analysis makes such reviews amenable to replication. This is especially important when scholars come forth who may be skeptical of the results of the meta-analysis. These researchers may take the blueprint of coding decisions from the original meta-analysis, make any changes or additions they may deem necessary, and re-do the analysis themselves. And related to the advantage of public coding decisions, the database for a meta-analysis is not static, but rather it is dynamic. As new studies are published, they can be added to the database of empirical studies. Upon doing so, the empirical relationships formerly under investigation may be reassessed. The new analyses may also take into account any new methodological variations that may have emerged following the initial meta-analysis.

Criticisms of Meta-Analysis

It should also be noted that meta-analyses are not beyond criticism. Wolf (1986) noted that critics of the method tend to focus on two potential problems. First, academic journals (and their editors) may be biased in favor of statistically significant findings, and therefore literature reviews may not uncover every study of a particular hypothesis that has been conducted. Rosenthal (1979) referred to this as the "file drawer problem" due to the tendency of studies failing to reject the null hypothesis to be buried away in file drawers. This omission of null-model studies may limit the utility of meta-analyses that are conducted on published research only. Although this issue cannot be dismissed fully, the potential for bias in a given meta-analysis is contingent upon the research context the scholar is operating within—a point that will be elaborated more fully below.

The second potential problem, which tends to be the more serious of the two, is that well-done studies may be included with studies using less rigorous methodological designs (i.e., what is referred to as the "apples and oranges" problem), which may bias the overall effect size estimates of the analysis (Cohen 1977). The primary mechanism for minimizing this problem is to code each empirical study for methodological variations that could influence the effect size estimate(s) (e.g., see Glass, McGaw, and Smith 1981; Pratt 2002). Doing so is especially important when integrating the results of studies using correlational research designs. Statistical control, as opposed to experimental control, is typically used to assess key theoretical relationships in correlational designs (and in most criminal justice and criminological research). In turn, estimates of effect size from correlational designs may be contingent, at least in part, on which variables are used as statistical controls, on the composition of the sample, and on how theoretical variables are measured. Thus, controlling statistically such methodological variations across empirical studies becomes necessary for calculating valid and reliable mean effect size estimates.

Relatedly, a more general caution should be added that the quality of a meta-analysis depends on the quality of research on the topic being investigated. One advantage of using published research—as many meta-analysts have done—is that the research studies being analyzed have been vetted for quality by the review process. Still, this does not obviate the fact that measurement error marks virtually all social science research endeavors. To some extent, meta-analysis assumes that error that is idiosyncratic to individual studies is minimized as empirical relationships are examined across a large sample of studies. Of more concern, however, are methodological biases that are patterned. To address this possibility, one approach—just mentioned above—is to examine within the meta-analysis whether methodological factors (e.g., measuring a variable one way rather than another) condition the estimates of the effect size. For those who remain skeptical of the results of the meta-analysis—claiming, for example, that the quality of the sample of studies assessed is suspect—another option remains: probe the meta-analysis for potential shortcomings and then undertake a new, rigorous independent study that attempts to falsify or otherwise revise the conclusions supported by the meta-analysis. In this way, a meta-analysis may prove useful not only in organizing existing knowledge but also in prompting or otherwise guiding future empirical research.

When is a Meta-Analysis Most Useful?

Depending on the state of the literature in a given area, a meta-analysis is not always useful. For example, if the pool of studies in a body of literature is small in number, these studies can simply be read and evaluated by those doing work in that area. To draw an analogy to another type of criminological research, we tend not to ascribe special meaning to a study that calculates a mean crime rate across three cities, so why would we do so for a meta-analysis that synthesizes the results of three independent studies? Put differently, just because SPSS will calculate a mean effect size of an "N" of three does not, by definition, make that mean effect size useful. There are, however, certain conditions under which a meta-analysis can be enormously helpful in making sense of the results of a body of empirical research. Specifically, four types of questions are particularly "ripe" for a meta-analysis to be performed.

First, in an area of research with a large number of studies where the results are typically characterized by scholars as being "mixed," a meta-analysis can be undertaken to determine whether the heterogeneity in study results can be attributed to methodological variations across studies. Indeed, a valuable feature of meta-analysis is that it allows for the assessment of the extent to which certain key methodological factors may condition the outcomes rendered by theoretical variables. Considering these "moderating variables" is important because it has implications for whether the effect size estimates that are reported reflect empirical reality or are mainly a methodological artifact. For example, a recent meta-analysis by Pratt et al. (in press) of 133 tests of social learning theory was able to determine whether the effect sizes differed significantly according to whether the source of social influence was measured as peer versus parental reinforcements, whether studies separated versus combine components of social learning theory, whether studies included statistical controls for variables specified by competing theories, and whether studies were cross-sectional versus longitudinal, and so on. It is this type of detailed methodological analysis for which meta-analysis, particularly, is well suited, and meta-analyses that explore relatively large bodies of literature in this way tend to be cited heavily in the years following their publication (Pratt and Cullen 2000).

Second, when there seems to be universal agreement among scholars concerning the empirical status of a research question, a meta-analysis of that very literature may appear to add nothing of substance to the field. And while this can certainly be true, it is equally true that a meta-analysis can be useful if its results are contrary to scholarly wisdom. A prime example of this can be seen in the case of the study by Andrews et al. (1990) on the effectiveness of correctional treatment. Their quantitative assessment of the literature challenged what had become an element of professional culture among criminologists that correctional rehabilitation "doesn't work" (see, e.g., the discussion by Cullen and Gendreau 2000). Thus, while it may certainly not always be the case, a meta-analysis—often more so than a single independent study or a narrative review—has the capacity to cause the field to re-think what is "known" about a particular body of research.

Third, and relatedly, meta-analyses are extremely useful when assessing literature that contains some form of intervention—whether it be a correctional intervention with offenders or a policy intervention intended to reduce crime rates—to give a more complete picture of whether that intervention "works," and there is a long history of meta-analysts diligently exploring these very kinds of questions (see Wells 2009). What is becoming more and more common—and more and more useful, however—are those meta-analyses that go beyond the question of "whether" and intervention works to instead uncover the conditions under which an intervention tends to work best. Along these lines, seminal pieces in correctional rehabilitation (see Lipsey 1992) were largely responsible for sparking the development of the "principles of effective intervention" with offenders in a correctional rehabilitation context (see also Pratt 2009), and more recent work has assessed the conditions under which policy interventions to reduce gun violence are most likely to be successful (Makarios and Pratt, in press).

Finally, a recent trend in the criminological literature has been to use meta-analysis to determine whether particular relationships between certain criminogenic risk factors and criminal behavior are large enough that we need to be able to explain them theoretically. These studies have built on earlier work such as Tittle, Villemez, and Smith's (1978) assessment of the SES-delinquency link and Walters' (1992) meta-analysis of the gene-crime relationship. Following their lead, recent studies have assessed the relationship between attention deficit hyperactivity disorder and crime/deviance (Pratt et al. 2002), as well as the effect of maternal cigarette smoking on crime and deviance in children (Pratt et al. 2006)—both of which were used to inform future research and criminological theory development within the self-control and neuropsychological deficit traditions (see, e.g., Gottfredson and Hirschi 1990; Moffitt 1993). Interestingly, both of these meta-analyses ended up sparking additional independent studies on these topics that have moved the state of the field even further (McGloin, Pratt, and Piquero 2006; Unnever, Cullen, and Pratt 2003)—something that meta-analyses, if done well, can be particularly adept at doing.

Thinking About Publication Bias

One of the issues in meta-analysis that is almost taken as an article of faith is that using only published work in a meta-analysis will bring with it a certain degree of controversy over the potential inferential errors that could be made concerning "publication bias" (see Rosenthal 1979). In particular, there is a near-religious commitment found within the meta-analysis literature that mean effect size estimates in a meta-analysis may be inflated because of the tendency of studies revealing non-significant relationships to be more likely to be either rejected for publication or to remain unsubmitted to journals by authors. This concern certainly has intuitive appeal, and the results of studies assessing publication bias in certain fields are widely available (Egger and Smith 1998); thus, in most cases meta-analysts would do well to take this concern seriously and to follow the methods that have been outlined thus far for detecting publication bias and adjusting for its potential effects (see Duval and

Tweedie 2000; Egger, Smith, Schneider, and Minder 1997). Nevertheless, adhering to a fundamentalist view of publication bias is problematic for three reasons.

First, should a meta-analyst make the decision to treat publication as a proxy for research quality, it is legitimate to question whether there is a supply of unpublished studies of high quality with null results lingering about in criminologists' file cabinets. To be sure, given the conditions for tenure and promotion in academic settings, criminologists have little incentive to leave a high-quality test of a theory in the file cabinet (see the discussion by Steiner and Schwartz 2006). Critics may be correct, however, in noting that published studies vary in their methodological quality. Using publication as a proxy for quality thus fails to address this variation *within published studies*. Yet, as noted above, this issue can be addressed with the use of moderator variables that can be coded across studies.

Second, and relatedly, the issue of unpublished studies needs to be placed in its appropriate academic context. Meta-analysis was primarily used to assess the effects of "treatments"—whether in medicine, psychology, education, or interventions with offenders (Hunt 1999). In these domains, those conducting the treatment interventions were not necessarily academics and therefore were not necessarily committed to publishing their work. Many evaluations were carried out to inform state and other agencies as to the effectiveness of a treatment strategy. As a result, it was commonplace for many evaluations, including some high-quality ones, not to appear in print. The *potential* bias of not including unpublished studies thus was high. Meta-analysts working within this area should therefore be cognizant of this potential problem. By contrast, in tests of criminological theories, those carrying out the research are almost exclusively academic criminologists (either in sociology or criminal justice). In almost all cases, the motivation for undertaking studies and writing up the results is to seek publication. Although it is conceivable that some high-quality studies have been relegated to the file drawer, it strains credulity to believe that there is a large supply of high-quality tests of criminological theories that exist and, if not included in the meta-analysis, would meaningfully bias the results of a meta-analysis.

Third, a related concern is that using unpublished studies introduces a whole set of biases that are difficult, if impossible, to control for. There is no way to establish the population of unpublished studies, there is no way to randomly sample those studies, or to know what one's "response rate" of unpublished studies is; thus, the statistical methods available for uncovering selection bias (see Bushway, Johnson, and Slocum 2007) are inapplicable in a meta-analysis context. Even among those who are contacted and asked to send a study, there is no way of knowing what the selection bias is (those who send you their research may be different from those who do not send their research). Using unpublished studies may therefore yield more studies, but the resulting biases may do more to distort the results than to provide a more accurate reflection of empirical reality.

In addition, the two works that scholars typically cite as evidence of the potential problem of publication bias in the social sciences are quite problematic themselves. For example, Cooper, DeNeve, and Charlton's (1997) survey of 33 psychologists found that "null findings" (which was not a mutually exclusive response category in their survey) were actually rarely invoked as an explanation among scholars for why they believed their work was not eventually published—lack of researcher interest and methodological problems were by far the most common reasons cited by their respondents. Second, Gerber and Malhotra's (2008) assessment of publication bias in sociology journals was only able to assess 14% of the studies that were originally gathered. Indeed, the remaining 86% of those studies failed to meet the inclusion criteria necessary for the statistical method the authors chose to use. Thus, as Pratt et al. (in press) recently pointed out, in an odd bit of methodological irony, it is difficult for Gerber and Malhotra (2008) to rule out in their own study the very form of publication bias that they were trying to expose.

As a final note on the issue of publication bias in meta-analysis, scholars have noted that such bias is potentially a greater threat in research involving clinical trials (see Dickersin, Min, and Meinert 1992), yet even a large-scale study of 745 manuscripts submitted to the *Journal of the American Medical Association* found "no significant difference in publication rates between those with positive vs negative results" (Olson et al. 2002, p. 2825). Thus, the issue of publication bias for meta-analysis—even in a context where the risk of its presence is should be at its peak—is far from a "given."

Bivariate Versus Multivariate Effect Sizes

Two possible proxies of an effect size estimate exist when combining the results of studies in a meta-analysis. The first option is to use bivariate statistics like correlation coefficients (Hedges and Olkin 1985), which are typically drawn from each empirical study's correlation matrix (assuming one is provided) or from a test statistic from an experimental or quasi-experimental research design.[2] The most significant problem with using such estimates, particularly in correlational research designs of course, is that of failing to account for partial spuriousness. Since the potential influences of other predictors of a dependent variable have not been removed, the bivariate correlation between two variables is at a substantial risk of being inflated.

2. Others in this tradition have used similar bivariate effect size estimates such as the Cohen's *d*, which is the difference between two group means divided by the pooled within-group standard deviation (Cohen 1977; see also Loeber and Stouthamer-Loeber 1986). Still other researchers have used the RIOC statistic (relative improvement over chance), which scales down certain descriptive statistics into a 2×2 table of whether or not a predictor variable is present and whether or not an individual engaged in delinquency (Loeber and Dishion 1983). Both of these statistics, however, assume, at minimum, a quasi-experimental research design, and are therefore not applicable to synthesizing correlational research based on statistical control.

This fact has certainly not been lost on criminologists, who typically deal with correlational research designs. Indeed, the norm in tests of criminological theories, for example, is to control statistically for potentially confounding variables in order to isolate the effects of the independent variables specified by a theory and to avoid model misspecification error. The implication of this approach for the quantitative synthesis of such studies is that an alternative effect size estimate may be used such as standardized regression coefficients from multivariate statistical models (see Paternoster 1987; Pratt 1998; Pratt and Cullen 2000; Tittle et al. 1978).

As but one example, standardized regression coefficients (beta weights) share certain properties with bivariate correlation coefficients (e.g., boundaries of 0 and 1/−1, assumptions about the skewness of the sampling distribution), which are largely due to their similarity in mathematical construction. Both are produced by the following equation:

$$\beta \text{ and } r = b\left[\frac{S_i}{S_d}\right]$$

In this equation, both the beta weight (β) and the correlation coefficient (r) are calculated as a linear slope estimate (b) standardized by the ratio of the standard deviations of the independent and dependent variables (Blalock 1972; Hanushek and Jackson 1977). The central difference between the beta weight and zero-order correlation coefficient values, then, is that the magnitude of the slope estimate generally decreases from the bivariate to the multivariate model because the variation in the dependent variable explained by other factors has been removed (the ratio of standard deviations stays the same from the r to the β estimates). Accordingly, using beta weights as an effect size estimate (at least for the meta-analysis of criminological research) may produce more valid mean effect size estimates than the inflated coefficients calculated from bivariate correlations because the issue of spuriousness has already been dealt with accordingly.

Nevertheless, the zero-order correlation effect size estimates may possibly be defended by acknowledging that the bivariate estimates are inflated. This may not be a cause for concern because even though the mean effect size estimates themselves may be inflated, the *relative rank-order* of the magnitudes of the effect sizes of various predictors should be the same. Thus, in the context of the criminological research, taking this position would require making a random-error assumption that model misspecification plagues *all predictors of any given outcome in the same way*. In other words, failing to control for a significant predictor of a dependent variable is assumed to have the effects of random error across all predictors from all studies; the mean effect size estimates should remain uncontaminated and therefore identical in their *relative* aggregated magnitude (Hedges and Olkin 1985).

There is little reason to believe, however, that this assumption will ever be met, since least-squares and maximum likelihood multivariate estimation techniques all begin with the basic understanding that model misspecification error contains, by definition, a systematic error component that cannot be treated solely as random fluctuations across studies that affect all predictors in exactly the same way (Hanushek and Jackson 1977). Supporters of using multivariate effect size estimates when synthesizing non-experimental research recognize this fact (see, e.g., Raudenbush et al. 1988). Accordingly, they tend to view zero-order relationships as, at best, limited in their substantive meaning and, at worst, dangerously misleading (Pratt et al., in press). This logic may even be extended to the suspicion that meta-analysts who choose to use bivariate correlation coefficients as effect size estimates when the beta weight alternative is present are either unaware of—or unconcerned with—how their results are polluted by systematic error.[3]

Nevertheless, a potential problem is that multivariate effect sizes will vary within datasets according to the unique ways in which statistical models are specified (i.e., how the variance-covariance matrix will vary according to the specific set of covariates in a multivariate model; see Hanushek and Jackson 1977). Since it is a practical impossibility to develop a coding scheme that would fully capture every permutation of model specification across every study in a body of literature, critics of the use of multivariate effect sizes have contended that the estimation problems associated with variations in model specification are insurmountable (see, e.g., Hedges and Olkin 1985). Recent methodological developments and software availability, however, have allowed meta-analysts to accommodate the variations in effect sizes introduced by differences in multivariate model specification by treating such variation as unobserved heterogeneity, which can be modeled statistically and incorporated into the calculation of overall effect size estimates (Pratt et al. 2006).

To do so, a correction for these potential sources of bias involves calculating mean effect size estimates using a multilevel modeling strategy (HLM 6.06). The HLM multilevel modeling program offers analyses called "Variance-Known" (or simply "V-Known") models for analyzing meta-analytic data (see Hox 1995; Raudenbush and Bryk 2002). Individual effect sizes are specified as the Level 1 units and the studies from which the effect sizes were derived are treated as Level 2 units such that effect sizes are nested within studies. The variances for individual effect sizes are computed[4] and entered into the HLM model. Study

3. Hedges and Olkin's critique of using multivariate effect sizes in meta-analysis was certainly valid when it was raised over two decades ago. Since then, however, advances in both quantitative methods and computer software (in particular, Hierarchical Linear Modeling methods and software) have resulted in new approaches for handling this potential problem in methodologically defensible ways, including the approach taken here.

4. The Level 1 effect size variances are computed using the formula for estimating the standard error of the Fisher *r*-to-*z* transformation (see, e.g., Hox 1995; Lipsey and Wilson 2001):

$$\sigma_1^2 = \frac{1}{(n_i - 3)}$$

The full model is estimated with the equation:

$$z_j = \gamma_0 + \gamma_1(\text{study } n) + \gamma_2(\text{number of effect sizes}) + u_j + e_j.$$

characteristics can be entered as Level 2 covariates to control for their possible impacts upon effect sizes. In short, while these methods are somewhat complex analytically, they are by no means impossible to master for the meta-analyst wishing to synthesize multivariate effect size estimates when the research context clearly calls for it.

Conclusions

In criminal justice and criminology, independent studies have to be conducted and presented rigorously in order to get published in the leading peer-reviewed journals in the field. In addition to the "art" of specifying an interesting research question and justifying it in the context of the existing literature, the "science" has to be up to snuff: data sources have to be specified, appropriate, and well-justified; measures have to demonstrate validity and reliability; statistical models need to be appropriately specified and conducted according to methodological norms; and results have to be interpreted correctly. The failure to attend to any of these issues makes scholars vulnerable to having their work rejected by journal editors.

Despite the care that is necessary in the production of original social science research, reviews of these same studies, however, are often sloppy by comparison in that they rarely are forced to adhere to such strict methodological standards. In response to the apparent paradox of the traditional narrative review of scientific literature having been typically conducted in an unscientific manner, Glass et al. (1981) contended that the technique of meta-analysis can bring the same level of analytical and methodological rigor found in independent studies to the literature review. The authors argued that "Contemporary research reviewing should be more technical and statistical than it is narrative ... The findings of multiple studies should be regarded as a complex data set, no more comprehensible without statistical analysis than would hundreds of data points in one study" (Glass et al. 1981, p. 12).

This call has been heeded only to a limited extent in criminal justice and criminology. It is still the normative practice to undertake a narrative-review approach with regard to most research areas, including the criminal justice policy literature (Walker 1994; Walker, Spohn, and Delone 1996) and the empirical status of criminological theories (Akers 2000; Burton and Cullen 1992; Kempf 1993; Lilly, Cullen, and Ball 2002). There is, however, an emerging trend toward quantitatively synthesizing existing knowledge in criminal justice and criminology through meta-analysis. Not everyone sees this as a good thing (Logan and Gaes 1993), yet meta-analysis can help to move us beyond clinical speculation about what a body of literature "really says" about its subject matter in a way that narrative reviews of literature really cannot.

Perhaps most importantly, there is still considerable room for meta-analyses to inform theory development in criminal justice and criminology. In the end, criminologists have remained either faithful to, or critical of, particular theories about the way the world works—whether it be offending behavior or how the criminal justice system responds to such behavior—for a host of reasons. A given theory may hold the allegiance of scholars for reasons associated with their social and/or political preferences (Gould 1996), the ease with which it can be tested and translated into publications (and therefore professional advancement, see Cole 1975), and even perhaps loyalty to one's intellectual mentors (see Pratt et al., in press). We would hope, however, that as criminal justice and criminology mature as a social science disciplines, the *empirical status* of the theory would carry at least as much weight, if not more, than these other criteria for what constitutes a "good" theory. And to that end, meta-analysis certainly should not be seen as the only method of establishing the empirical status of a body of literature, yet as a tool for doing so its use has proven to be a welcome addition to the criminologists' toolbox.

References

Akers, R. L. 2000. *Criminological theories: Introduction and evaluation* (2d ed.). Los Angeles, CA: Roxbury.

Andrews, D. A., I. Zinger, R. D. Hoge, J. Bonta, P. Gendreau, and F. T. Cullen. 1990. Does correctional treatment work? A clinically relevant and psychologically informed meta-analysis. *Criminology* 28: 369-404.

Blalock, H. M. 1972. *Social statistics* (2nd ed.). New York: McGraw-Hill.

Bonta, J., M. Law, and K. Hanson. 1998. The prediction of criminal and violent recidivism among mentally disordered offenders: A meta-analysis. *Psychological Bulletin* 123: 123-142.

Burton, V. S. Jr., and F. T. Cullen. 1992. The empirical status of strain theory. *Journal of Crime and Justice* 15: 1-30.

Bushway, S., B. Johnson, and L. Slocum. 2007. Is the magic still there? The relevance of the Heckman two-step correction for selection bias in criminology. *Journal of Quantitative Criminology* 23: 151-178.

Chiricos, T. G. 1987. Rates of crime and unemployment: An analysis of aggregate research evidence. *Social Problems* 34: 187-212.

Cohen, J. 1977. *Statistical power analysis for the behavioral sciences* (Rev. ed.). New York: Academic Press.

Cole, S. 1975. The growth of scientific knowledge: Theories of deviance as a case study. In L. A. Coser (Ed.), *The idea of social structure: Papers in honor of Robert K. Merton* (pp. 175-200). New York: Harcourt Brace Jovanovich.

Cooper, H., K. DeNeve, and K. Charlton. 1997. Finding the missing science: The fate of studies submitted for review by a human subjects committee. *Psychological Methods* 2: 447-452.

Cullen, F. T., and P. Gendreau. 2000. Assessing correctional rehabilitation: Policy, practice, and prospects. In J. Horney (Ed.), *Criminal justice 2000: Vol. 3. Policies, processes, and decisions of the criminal justice system*. Washington, DC: U.S. Department of Justice, National Institute of Justice.

Daly, K., and R. L. Bordt. 1995. Sex effects and sentencing: An analysis of the statistical literature. *Justice Quarterly* 12: 141-174.

Dickersin, K., Y.-I. Min, and C. L. Meinert. 1992. Factors influencing publication of research results: Follow-up of applications submitted to two institutional review boards. *Journal of the American Medical Association* 267: 374-378.

Duval, S., and R. Tweedie. 2000. Trim and fill: A simple funnel-plot-based method of testing and adjusting for publication bias in meta-analysis. *Biometrics* 56: 455-463.

Egger, M., and G. D. Smith. 1998. Meta-analysis bias in location and selection of studies. *British Medical Journal* 316: 61-66.

Egger, M., G. D. Smith, M. Schneider, and C. Minder. 1997. Bias in meta-analysis detected by a simple, graphical test. *British Medical Journal* 315: 629-634.

Franklin, T. W., C. A. Franklin, and T. C. Pratt. 2006. Examining the empirical relationship between prison crowding and inmate misconduct: A meta-analysis of conflicting research results. *Journal of Criminal Justice* 34: 401-412.

Gendreau, P., T. Little, and C. E. Goggin. 1996. A meta-analysis of the predictors of adult offender recidivism: What works! *Criminology* 34: 575-607.

Gerber, A. S., and N. Malhotra. 2008. Publication bias in empirical sociological research: Do arbitrary significance levels distort published results? *Sociological Methods and Research* 37: 3-30.

Glass, G. V. 1977. Integrating findings: The meta-analysis of research. *Review of Research in Education* 5: 351-379.

Glass, G. V., B. McGaw, and M. L. Smith. 1981. *Meta-analysis in social research.* Beverly Hills, CA: Sage.

Gottfredson, M. R., and T. Hirschi. 1990. *A general theory of crime.* Palo Alto, CA: Stanford University Press.

Gould, S. J. 1996. *The mismeasure of man* (Rev. ed.). New York: W.W. Norton.

Hanushek, E. A., and J. E. Jackson. 1977. *Statistical methods for social scientists.* San Diego, CA: Academic Press.

Hedges, L. V., and I. Olkin. 1985. *Statistical methods for meta-analysis.* Orlando, FL: Academic Press.

Hox, J. J. 1995. *Applied multilevel analysis.* Amsterdam: T.T. Publikaties.

Hubbard, D., and T. C. Pratt. 2002. A meta-analysis of the predictors of delinquency among girls. *Journal of Offender Rehabilitation* 34: 1-13.

Hunt, M. 1999. *How science takes stock: The story of meta-analysis.* New York: Russell Sage.

Hunter, J. E., and F. L. Schmidt. 1996. Cumulative research knowledge and social policy formulation: The critical role of meta-analysis. *Psychology, Public Policy, and Law* 2: 324-347.

Hunter, J. E., F. L. Schmidt, and G. B. Jackson. 1982. *Meta-analysis: Culminating research findings across studies.* Beverly Hills, CA: Sage.

Izzo, R., and R. R. Ross. 1990. Meta-analysis of rehabilitation programs for juvenile delinquents. *Criminal Justice and Behavior* 17: 134-142.

Kempf, K. L. 1993. The empirical status of Hirschi's control theory. In F. Adler and W. S. Laufer (Eds.), *New directions in criminological theory: Advances in criminological theory* (Vol. 4, pp. 143-185). New Brunswick, NJ: Transaction.

Lab, S. P., and J. T. Whitehead. 1990. From "nothing works' to the "appropriate works": The latest stop on the search for the secular grail. *Criminology* 28: 405-417.

Light, R., and P. V. Smith. 1971. Accumulating evidence: Procedures for resolving contradictions among different research studies. *Harvard Educational Review* 41: 429-471.

Lilly, J. R., F. T. Cullen, and R. A. Ball. 2007. *Criminological theory: Context and consequences* (4th ed.). Thousand Oaks, CA: Sage.

Lipsey, M. W. 1992. Juvenile delinquency treatment: A meta-analytic inquiry into the variability of effects. In T. D. Cook et al. (Eds.), *Meta-analysis for explanation: A casebook* (pp. 83-127). New York: Russell Sage.

Lipsey, M. W. 2003. Those confounded moderators in meta-analysis: Good, bad, and ugly. *Annals of the American Academy of Political and Social Science* 587: 69-81.

Lipsey, M. W., and D. B. Wilson. 1993. The efficacy of psychological, educational, and behavioral treatment: Confirmation from meta-analysis. *American Psychologist* 48: 1181-1209.

Lipsey, M. W., and D. B. Wilson. 2001. *Practical meta-analysis.* Thousand Oaks, CA: Sage.

Loeber, R., and T. J. Dishion. 1983. Early predictors of male delinquency: A review. *Psychological Bulletin* 94: 68-99.

Loeber, R., and M. Stouthamer-Loeber. 1986. Family factors as correlates and predictors of juvenile conduct problems and delinquency. In M. Tonry and N. Morris (Eds.), *Crime and justice: An annual review of research* (Vol. 7, pp. 29-149). Chicago, IL: University of Chicago Press.

Logan, C. H., and G. G. Gaes. 1993. Meta-analysis and the rehabilitation of punishment. *Justice Quarterly* 10: 245-263.

Makarios, M. D., and T. C. Pratt. In press. The effectiveness of policies and programs that attempt to reduce gun violence: A meta-analysis. *Crime and Delinquency.*

McGloin, J. M., T. C. Pratt, and A. Piquero. 2006. A life-course analysis of the criminogenic effects of maternal cigarette smoking during pregnancy: A research note on the mediating impact of neuropsychological deficit. *Journal of Research in Crime and Delinquency* 43: 412-426.

Moffitt, T. E. 1993. Adolescent-limited and life-course-persistent antisocial behavior: A developmental taxonomy. *Psychological Review* 100: 674-701.

Niemi, R. G. 1986. Series editor's introduction. In F. M. Wolf (Ed.), *Meta-analysis: Quantitative methods for research synthesis* (pp. 5-6). Newbury Park, CA: Sage.

Olson, C. M., D. Rennie, D. Cook, K. Dickersin, A. Flanagin, J. W. Hogan, et al. 2002. Publication bias in editorial decision making. *Journal of the American Medical Association* 287: 2825-2828.

Paternoster, R. 1987. The deterrent effect of the perceived certainty of punishment: A review of the evidence and issues. *Justice Quarterly* 4: 173-217.

Piehl, A. M. 1998. Economic conditions, work, and crime. In M. Tonry (Ed.), *The handbook of crime and punishment* (pp. 302-322). New York: Oxford University Press.

Pillemer, D. B., and R. Light. 1980. Synthesizing outcomes: How to use research evidence from many studies. *Harvard Educational Review* 50: 176-195.

Pratt, T. C. 1998. Race and sentencing: A meta-analysis of conflicting empirical research results. *Journal of Criminal Justice* 26: 513-524.

Pratt, T. C. 2002. Meta-analysis and its discontents: Treatment destruction techniques revisited. *Journal of Offender Rehabilitation* 35: 23-40.

Pratt, T. C. 2009. *Addicted to incarceration: Corrections policy and the politics of misinformation in the United States.* Thousand Oaks, CA: Sage.

Pratt, T. C., and F. T. Cullen. 2000. The empirical status of Gottfredson and Hirschi's general theory of crime: A meta-analysis. *Criminology* 38: 931-964.

Pratt, T. C., and F. T. Cullen. 2005. Assessing macro-level predictors and theories of crime: A meta-analysis. In M. Tonry (Ed.), *Crime and justice: A review of research* (Vol. 32, pp. 373-450). Chicago, IL: University of Chicago Press.

Pratt, T. C., F. T. Cullen, K. R. Blevins, L. E. Daigle, and T. D. Madensen. 2006. The empirical status of deterrence theory: A meta-analysis. In F. T. Cullen, J. P. Wright, and K. R. Blevins (Eds.), *Taking stock: The status of criminological theory, advances in criminological theory* (Vol. 15, pp. 367-396). New Brunswick, NJ: Transaction.

Pratt, T. C., F. T. Cullen, K. R. Blevins, L. Daigle, and J. D. Unnever. 2002. The relationship of attention deficit hyperactivity disorder to crime and delinquency: A meta-analysis. *International Journal of Police Science and Management* 4: 344-360.

Pratt, T. C., F. T. Cullen, C. S. Sellers, L. T. Winfree, T. Madensen, L. Daigle, et al. In press. The empirical status of social learning theory: A meta-analysis. *Justice Quarterly.*

Pratt, T. C., and C. T. Lowenkamp. 2002. Conflict theory, economic conditions, and homicide: A time series analysis. *Homicide Studies* 6: 61-83.

Pratt, T. C., and J. Maahs. 1999. Are private prisons more cost-effective than public prisons? A meta-analysis of evaluation research studies. *Crime and Delinquency* 45: 358-372.

Pratt, T. C., J. M. McGloin, and N. E. Fearn. 2006. Maternal cigarette smoking during pregnancy and criminal/deviant behavior: A meta-analysis. *International Journal of Offender Therapy and Comparative Criminology* 50: 672-690.

Raudenbush, S. W., B. J. Becker, and H. Kalaian. 1988. Modeling multivariate effect sizes. *Psychological Bulletin* 103: 111-120.

Raudenbush, S. W., and A. S. Bryk. 2002. *Hierarchical linear models: Applications and data analysis methods* (2nd ed.). Thousand Oaks, CA: Sage.

Rosenthal, R. 1979. The "file drawer problem" and tolerance for null results. *Psychological Bulletin* 65: 185-193.

Shaffer, D. K., and T. C. Pratt. 2009. Meta-analysis, moderators, and treatment effectiveness: The importance of digging deeper for evidence of program integrity. *Journal of Offender Rehabilitation* 48: 101-119.

Steiner, B., and J. Schwartz. 2006. The scholarly productivity of institutions and their faculty in leading criminology and criminal justice journals. *Journal of Criminal Justice* 34: 393-400.

Tittle, C. R., W. J. Villemez, and D. A. Smith. 1978. The myth of social class and criminality: An empirical assessment of the empirical evidence. *American Sociological Review* 43: 643-656.

Unnever, J. D., F. T. Cullen, and T. C. Pratt. 2003. Parental management, ADHD, and delinquent involvement: Reassessing Gottfredson and Hirschi's general theory. *Justice Quarterly* 20: 471-500.

Walker, S. 1994. *Sense and nonsense about crime and drugs* (3rd ed.). Belmont, CA: Wadsworth.

Walker, S., C. Spohn, and M. Delone. 1996. *The color of justice: Race, ethnicity, and crime in America.* Belmont, CA: Wadsworth.

Walters, G. D. 1992. A meta-analysis of the gene-crime relationship. *Criminology* 30: 595-613.

Wells, E. 2009. Uses of meta-analysis in criminal justice research: A quantitative review. *Justice Quarterly* 26: 268-294.

Whatley, M. A. 1996. Victim characteristics influencing attributions of responsibility to rape victims: A meta-analysis. *Aggression and Violent Behavior* 1: 81-95.

Whitehead, J. T., and S. P. Lab. 1989. A meta-analysis of juvenile correctional treatment. *Journal of Research in Crime and Delinquency* 26: 276-295.

Wolf, F. M. 1986. *Meta-analysis: Quantitative methods for research synthesis.* Thousand Oaks, CA: Sage.

An Overview of Social Network Analysis

Jean Marie McGloin and David S. Kirk

Social network analysis refers both to a view that social relations provide crucial insight to human behavior and to a set of analytic tools that enable the study of these social relations. Both practitioners and theorists interested in crime can gain important knowledge from a focus on social networks, as the growing literature in criminology demonstrates. This article provides an introduction for scholars interested in becoming better versed in the concepts of basic social network concepts and techniques, as well as a discussion about the conditions under which this form of analysis may be particularly useful.

Introduction

Social network analysis is an orientation towards the understanding of human behavior that focuses on the importance of social relations. It is also a set of tools that enable the investigation of social relations and their consequence. The underlying basis of social network analysis is that individuals are interdependent, and these interdependencies have consequences for behavior. In contrast, social scientists have traditionally conceived of individuals as independent units, and have limited their focus to the role of actor attributes and norms as explanatory variables of behavior.

Theoretically, there are numerous reasons to draw upon core social network concepts to explain the etiology of criminal behavior. Warr (2002, p. 3) argues that, "criminal conduct is predominantly social behavior. Most offenders are imbedded in a network of friends who also break the law, and the single strongest predictor of criminal behavior known to criminologists is the number of delinquent friends an individual has." Consistent with this view, several seminal works in criminology highlight the group nature of delinquency, showing that the average delinquent committed his acts while in the company of accomplices (Cloward and Ohlin 1960; Cohen 1955; Shaw and McKay [1942]1969; Short and Strodtbeck 1965). This observation is echoed in Sutherland's (1947) differential association theory, which posits that criminal behavior is learned through social interaction in intimate groups.

The salience of social networks does not cease once scholars turn attention away from peer effects. Indeed, social networks also play important roles in theories of social control (Hirschi 1969), social disorganization, and collective efficacy (Sampson and Groves 1989; Sampson, Raudenbush, and Earls 1997), as well as opportunity perspectives (Osgood, Wilson, and O'Malley 1996). Network analysis also holds utility outside theoretical inquiries. Several scholars have suggested that network analysis can be a powerful tool for law enforcement investigations that seek to understand crime problems (Coady 1985; Davis 1981; Howlett 1980; McGloin 2005b), as well as for the development of interventions and suppression tactics (Braga, Kennedy, Waring, and Piehl 2001; McGloin 2005b). Thus, one could rightly argue that being familiar with methods that can appropriately capture and describe social networks is essential for criminological scholars as well as practitioners.

Though social network analysis may be relatively novel to criminologists, it is not a new technique or viewpoint. According to Scott (2000), social network analysis grew out of three traditions. First, cognitive and social psychologists of the 1930s, working under the gestalt paradigm, researched the structure of groups as well as the information flow among the members. Second, Harvard anthropologists sought to study and refine the premises of anthropologist A.R. Radcliffe-Brown by focusing on interpersonal relations and sub-groups within social networks. Third, researchers at Manchester University examined on tribal societies, using these studies to further refine social theory and the study of community relations. While Radcliffe-Brown was also the primary influence for the Manchester researchers, their studies tended to focus on conflict and change rather than cohesion, which served as the focus for the Harvard group (Scott 2000). Collectively, these streams of research, which led to theoretical, methodological, and analytical maturity and refinement, serve as the foundation for network analysis (Wasserman and Faust 1994).

With these theoretical and practical motivations in mind, the aim of this article is to present a blueprint for the application of social network analysis in the study of crime. To proceed, we first provide a brief overview of characteristics of network data and then describe the array of analytical techniques, both descriptive and inferential, that network analysis has to offer.

Network Data

The unit of analysis in social network studies is the relationship between nodes (i.e., the links among individuals, groups, or other objects). This contrasts traditional studies of behavior, which typically analyze the attributes of individuals to determine the characteristics of individuals who engage in certain acts such as crime. To be clear about the distinction between attributional and relational data, consider the following contrast: the extent of deviant norms a person reports is an attribute of the person, whereas the intensity or frequency of communication about these norms among his friends would be an exchange relationship.

Thus, scholars interested in using social network analysis require data on the ties among entities (i.e., the links among the nodes). This tie or link can take many forms, such as friendship, co-membership, communication, and shared behavior.[1] Depending upon the nature of the links, as well as the research questions guiding the investigation, these relational ties can be undirected or directed. Examples of undirected, or mutual, ties would include siblings, married partners, or an affiliation tie such as two individuals belonging to the same street gang. Directed ties include identifying someone as a friend and receiving a call in a wiretapping ring; there is a flow or direction to the relationship. Directed data may be uniquely important for some criminological questions of interest, perhaps in terms of directing policy (e.g., who is "organizing" the illegal market by initiating and handling contact and product exchange?) or stimulating research questions (e.g., is there a difference between someone who has reciprocal deviant friends and someone who is not viewed as a mutual friend by deviant peers).

It is important to note that the links among nodes can also have value. For example, researchers may code relations according to some level of attachment or involvement (e.g., number of days per week two individuals communicate). These values may reflect a continuous measure or scale, they can be categorical, reflecting distinct relations (i.e., friends versus siblings), or some combination thereof. The latter example is also known as a multirelational network (i.e., two nodes may be tied together in multiple ways), which can shed insight on how connected or "intimately related" units are (e.g., see Krohn's [1986] discussion of multiplexity). For instance, two individuals may be tied through blood relation and gang affiliation.

After a researcher decides what type of links he or she is interested in and collects network data, the information is stored in an adjacency matrix. In this matrix, the rows and columns are defined by the actors (i.e., nodes) in the network, and the cell values of the matrix indicate whether two actors are associated (i.e., adjacent).[2] In a binary matrix, the cell value indicates either the presence (a value of 1) or absence (a value of 0) of a tie. In a valued matrix, the cell values indicate the strength or intensity of the relationship between the two nodes. This matrix serves as the information base for analysis (Wasserman and Faust 1994).

By focusing on relational data, network analysis implicitly assumes that the quantity and quality of associations among individuals (or other units) have the potential to be powerful explanatory factors for a variety of social behaviors. In order to investigate this premise and provide empirical insight, network analysis relies on three mathematical foundations: (1) graph theory, (2) algebraic

1. Similarly, nodes can be of many different types, including individuals, organizations, countries, and groups.

2. In addition to adjacency matrices, there are also incident matrices, in which the rows are the nodes and the columns are incidents, events, or affiliations (i.e., the value in a cell would indicate whether a particular node was part of that specific incident, event, or affiliated with that specific group).

models, and (3) statistical/probability theory. From these foundations, scholars have acquired the language to describe social networks as well as numerous analytic options for quantifying and studying social structure (Wasserman and Faust 1994). For the purposes of this article, it is most beneficial if scholars think about potential analyses as falling into one of the three categories: descriptive graphs; network measures, and more advanced network modeling techniques.

Using Network Graphs

One of the primary contributions of network analysis is the "sociogram," in which individuals (or whatever nodes the investigation focuses on) are represented by points and social relations are represented by lines between the points (Moreno 1934). These lines can be amended to convey both directionality (by having arrows) and intensity of the relationship (varying levels of thickness or color). Maltz (1998, p. 400) argues that "when shown in graph forms data are displayed without assumption." Indeed, graphical displays of data have already demonstrated that studying social networks can shed important insight on crime patterns and criminal organizations (e.g., Finckenauer and Waring 1998; McGloin 2005a; Natarajan 2006), and consequently inform and guide policy (e.g., Kennedy, Braga, Piehl, and Waring 2001; McGloin 2005a; Tita, Riley, and Greenwood 2005). Advancements in knowledge of street gang structure have been particularly aided by the use of network graphs.

It certainly seems logical to view street gangs from a network perspective. On this point, Fleisher (2002, p. 200) notes, "gangs are social networks composed of individual gang members, and that gang member behavior is determined in part by a gang member's location in the structure of the social network." In other words, the dynamic nature of the relationships among gang members is a defining part of the organization and can exert a robust influence on the behavior of the group, both collectively and as individuals. Perhaps it is not surprising, then, that the social organization of street gangs has remained an empirical topic of interest for decades (Decker 2001). This is likely due to the fact that gang structure has criminogenic importance (i.e., as gangs become more cohesive, the exchange of deviant or criminal definitions becomes stronger and fosters more crime; see Klein 1971, 1995), as well as the fact that there is a divergence among data sources with regard to how organized street gangs typically are. The vast majority of empirical work suggests that the general gang landscape consists of transient, flexible, relatively flat, decentralized groups (Curry and Decker 2003; Decker 1996; Decker and Van Winkle 1994, 1996; Klein and Maxson 1994; Klein, Maxson, and Cunningham 1991), though a handful of scholars, as well as the general public, instead view street gangs as well-structured and entrepreneurial (Padilla 1992; Sanchez-Jankowski 1991; Skolnick, Correl, Navarro, and Rabb 1988; Taylor 1990).

Research on gang organization has traditionally asked gang members to report on the presence and importance of rules and meetings, internal discipline, and reported cohesion within the group (Cartwright, Howard, and Reuterman 1970; Decker 2001; Weisel 1999; Yablonsky 1962). This provides some insight into organization, but network analysis arguably provides more systematic and direct ways to investigate the structure of street gangs. In fact, one could assert that network analysis can address Klein's (1995, p. 103) call that, "we badly need more careful research on gang structures ... The gang phenomenon is complex, and it challenges us as social scientists and interested laypersons."

As an example, McGloin (2005a) used network analysis to gain insight about the social structure of four primary street gangs in Newark, New Jersey. Using experiential data from law enforcement, as well as other supplemental information, she constructed an adjacency matrix in which the nodes were gang members and the multirelational links captured five distinct relationships that could overlap (e.g., siblings and co-defendants). The sociograms emerging from this work demonstrated that none of the street gangs in Newark were cohesive; instead, all four networks were a fragmented assortment of smaller subgroups. Given this network structure, McGloin (2005a) warned against interventions that could increase group cohesion, thereby promoting more crime (see Klein 1971). Furthermore, the sociograms called attention to those gang members who serve as the bridge between subgroups, since they are vital to maintaining the overall connectedness of the network. From this graphical display of the data, she asserted that removing these "cut points" through police intervention might be particularly crippling or damaging to the overall gang (for other examples of network graphs, see Finckenauer and Waring 1998; Sarnecki 2001). At the minimum, she suggested, individuals who occupied these positions would be strategic choices for communication if law enforcement hoped to spread a deterrence message.

Research has also demonstrated that using graphs to understand the social structure among gangs, rather than within gangs, can be informative. Perhaps the best known example of this is the Boston Gun Project, which relied on network analysis in its problem analysis phase (Kennedy, Braga, and Piehl 1997). As part of its endeavor to study youth homicide, the Boston Gun Project gathered data on the area gangs that were especially problematic for the local neighborhoods and the law enforcement community (Braga et al. 2001; Kennedy et al. 1997, 2001). During the analysis phase, researchers produced sociograms in which the gangs served as the nodes and rivalries among the gangs served as the linkages. This analysis allowed the stakeholders to understand why particular geographic areas were experiencing violent conflict—largely because the gangs tied to those territories were those heavily embedded in conflictual relations with other gangs. This sociogram also illustrated what gangs were most integral to the network. Specifically, the gangs that had the most connections essentially nominated themselves for law enforcement focus and intervention. Rather than considering one gang set to the exclusion of the remainder of the landscape—a common strategy within law enforcement (Stelfox 1996)—the knowledge of the connections amongst the gangs provided unique leverage when undertaking the intervention strategy (see also Tita et al. 2005).

Constructing sociograms also provides insight for empirical investigations outside the realm of street gangs, including co-offending networks (McGloin and Piquero 2010; Sarnecki 2001) and organized crime (Coles 2001; McIllwain 1999). For instance, Finckenauer and Waring (1998) relied on network analysis when studying Russian émigré crime in the New York area, and Natarajan (2000) applied network analysis to data from wiretaps and prosecutorial information about a drug trafficking organization, also in New York. This afforded her insight into the structure of this criminal enterprise, as well clarified which individuals were central to the organization. Bunker and Sullivan (2001) argue that South American drug cartels are also adopting network structures, which allows them to expand connections and links in the legitimate business world. Given the various structures that such organizations can take, and the varied positions member may occupy, sociograms provide invaluable guidance for policy-makers and interventionists (e.g., RICO).

Using Network Measures

While a visual description of social networks has many important and practical applications, social network analysis is also useful for describing the properties of networks as well as testing hypotheses about the patterns of relationships in a network and the importance of these patterns for individual and group behavior. Such analytic tasks are facilitated through a broad array of social network measures. Some measures capture qualities of the network as a whole, such as density (i.e., cohesion). This measure not only provides a common metric across which scholars can systematically compare groups of varying size and type (i.e., whether certain ethnic organized groups are more cohesive than others) but it also provides a clear operationalization of a concept that may be an important predictor of group behavior (i.e., more cohesive gangs are responsible for more crime). Network analysis also contains an array of measures that can speak to an individual's position (or whatever the node is) in the network. For instance, network measures can identify which people are the most "popular" members of a network (i.e., in-degree) and to what degree communication in a network must "go through" certain individuals (i.e., between-ness centrality). Using these measures of the global network and positions within it is relevant to key areas of criminological interest and research.

For instance, the bulk of current work on social disorganization focuses on the density and extent of neighborhood networks, with the notion that they structure a neighborhood's capacity for social control. Empirical investigations confirm that social networks are weak and social controls are constrained in socially disorganized neighborhoods, leading to higher crime rates (Bursik 1986, 1988; Sampson and Groves 1989). Recent work even suggests that the network ties in neighborhoods can shape the type of crime that emerges (Schreck, McGloin, and Kirk 2009), harkening back to Cloward and Ohlin's

(1960) propositions, which recognized that opportunities for crime and for learning about crime were socially structured.

Perhaps the area that is best known for recently embracing network measures is the literature on peer influence. This research typically flows from the presumption that social relations are necessary for the transmission of norms, beliefs, and behavior. Learning theory (particularly differential association) orients us towards the importance of the following factors: (1) with whom a person associates; (2) the balance of individuals in the network (i.e., whether it is mostly deviant); (3) the transference of deviant norms through these links; and (4) the quality or strength of the associations (i.e., more frequent associations can have a greater impact on behavior). Criminologists working outside of a formal network framework undeniably have produced important work on peer influence, but a network approach has allowed an expansion in focus, leading scholars to recognize that the connectivity and cohesiveness among one's peers may be extremely consequential to the behavior of the focal individual.

For instance, recent empirical work has demonstrated that variations in the connectivity in a deviant social network, as well as social position in this network, tend to coincide with variations in offending. Haynie (2001) found that individuals who occupied more central positions in their deviant friendship networks had amplified levels of delinquency. This finding echoed the consistent observation that core gang members (individuals with high centrality in a deviant social network) tend to engage in more delinquency than do their counterparts who occupy more peripheral positions in the street gang network (Klein 1995; Peterson, Miller, and Esbensen 2001; see also Haynie 2001).

Haynie (2001) also incorporated the density of adolescent peer networks into an investigation of the criminogenic impact of deviant peers on delinquency. She found that being part of dense friendship networks amplified the deleterious effect of having deviant peers. This finding was consistent with a large body of work in network analysis that has examined the repercussions of group cohesion on the behavior of group members. The general conclusion of this literature is that we should expect relatively greater homogeneity in behavior (e.g., delinquency) within cohesive groups, largely because of the overwhelming connectedness of individuals in a dense network. As Smith (2005, p. 10) observed, "there is little that anyone can do without having others in the network discover their actions. This monitoring capacity is key if sanctions are to be imposed for noncompliance, and if members are to be kept in line." Under a learning framework, dense deviant groups provide a more intense exchange of criminal definitions and reinforcement contingencies, as well as reduce the influence of possibly prosocial "outsiders" (Granovetter 1973; Haynie 2001).

While the methods of social network analysis provide researchers the empirical tools to operationalize many concepts long core to theories of crime, network measures also enable new theoretical discoveries about the etiology of crime. In other words, such measures can capture extant criminological concepts more closely, but they can also serve as an important heuristic for how we think about crime and criminality. As an example, literature on social networks outside criminology often calls attention to weak ties and/or structural holes (Burt 1992; Granovetter 1973). Scholars have argued that nonredundant networks (i.e., networks in which there are many unique connections that are not redundant; networks with structural holes) open up an individual's exposure to diverse information, skills, and opportunities. This provides gains for social investment and promotes economic advancement and success. In contrast, individuals in redundant networks have a lower probability of leveraging their network for success, given that they tend to have access to repetitive information and opportunities (see also Davern and Hachen 2006; Lin 1982, 1990; Podolny and Baron 1997).

Morselli and Tremblay (2004) recently imported this concept to criminology, finding that offenders in less redundant networks had higher criminal earnings than did their counterparts in more redundant criminal networks. Thus, a concept and measure that provided insight into the role of social networks in the legitimate economic market is "translatable" to the illegitimate market. McGloin and Piquero (2010) also focused on network redundancy, though they adopted a more traditional criminological outcome of interest: offending specialization. They found that juvenile offenders whose co-offending networks were less redundant also tended to engage in a variety of crime types when offending with others, reflecting an exposure to more varied skills and opportunities. Alternatively, juveniles who had more redundant (i.e., more dense) co-offending networks tended to engage in the same kind of offense type when committing group crimes.

Using Network Modeling Techniques

Finally, network analysis also offers more advanced options than sociograms or descriptive measures, such as network autocorrelation models. These models are often used to capture social processes, such as the diffusion of ideas and innovation. Many empirical explanations for behavior, including criminal behavior, rely upon statistical methods which assume that individuals are independent units. If there is interdependency among the behaviors of individuals in a social network, researchers need an inferential strategy that accounts for this, given that estimates from a standard linear regression model will be biased. Network models explicitly account for the fact that there is interdependence among the nodes, much like how the use of hierarchical models, as well as random and fixed effects models, addresses clustering and interdependence. Admittedly, the extent of interdependence among subjects/nodes may be minimal in some network studies, but if the nodes cannot be assumed to be independent, then analytic methods that do assume independence may not be able to capture the true importance of group structure on behavior.

There are several models and techniques available to scholars interested in studying more complicated network dynamics. For those interested in these methods, we recommend reviewing Carrington, Scott, and Wasserman (2005),

Wasserman and Faust (1994), as well as Snijders' page on network analysis and related software (http://stat.gamma.rug.nl/siena.html). For a criminologically relevant example of network models, we call attention to Papachristos' (2009) research on gang homicide in Chicago. Papachristos (2009, p. 74) argues that "the social structure of gang murder is defined by the manner in which social networks are constructed and by people's placement in them" rather than individual-level attributes. Use of dyadic analysis to understand why a murder links certain gangs, as well as network autocorrelation models to study reciprocity, led him to conclude that gang conflict is like a contagion process in which groups negotiate social position and dominance through aggression and conflict.

Additional Data Considerations

Being aware of potential interdependencies in the data is important, but it is not the only data concern when using network analysis. Specifically, we would like to call attention to two data-related issues, if only to provide some caution and guidance. First, researchers should be thoughtful about their sampling procedures. Ideally, a social network is fully complete and reflects the entire population of interest. On some occasions, this is a reasonable goal for researchers, such as when studying a particular grade in a school or a business. In these cases, the population has clearly defined boundaries. In other cases, however, sampling becomes complicated, both conceptually and practically, because the boundary of the population is unclear. If one is interested in deviant peer networks or street gangs, for example, and begins sampling people in a school or on the street, in order to complete this network the researcher should follow-up each identified friend in what could be a never-ending snowball sample. At some point, the researcher must decide on when the boundary has been "met" and justify it accordingly. Ideally, this boundary should have conceptual merit, not simply be based on ease or previous work.

Scholars who are interested in ego-centric networks have similar sampling considerations. To be clear, ego-centric networks typically contain the people to whom the individual is connected (on whatever link(s) is of interest), as well as any links among these alters (i.e., nodes in the network other than the ego). This means that researchers who purport to capture subjects' ego-centric peer networks, yet limit subjects to the identification of only a handful of friends, may have problems with validity. One of the key attributes of the Add Health data is that in collecting friendship network data, it allowed subjects to identify up to five friends of each sex (which appears to have exhausted the size of the friendship network for most adolescents; see McGloin and Shermer 2009).[3]

Finally, most criminological inquiries wrestle with missing data and the varied techniques of how to manage it. In network studies, missing data can

3. See the following link for information on the Add Health data repository: http://www.cpc.unc.edu/projects/addhealth

have a sort of domino-effect. To illustrate this point, imagine a project that gathers network data for youth in a summer camp, asking about friendship links among the students. The researcher is interested in alcohol use within the students' personal networks (i.e., "egocentric" networks). If one student was absent on the day of the survey, of course there will be no friendship network data for him or her. Importantly, unlike with typical data, his absence can affect the degree to which other subjects have missing data. Though it arguably will not affect the structure of other students' basic networks, because they were able to identify him as a friend even though he was absent, it could impact the extent to which their peer group appears to engage in alcohol use. If drinking behavior among friends is based on the friends' self-reports, then if this absent student was identified as a friend in 20 networks, these 20 people now have missing data on whatever variable measures the extent of peer drinking. Under certain circumstances, therefore, the impact of missing data can quickly grow in network studies.

Concluding Remarks

As way of conclusion, it is instructive to again emphasize what is distinctive about social network analysis. Individuals in society are dependent upon each other, and social network analysis provides a framework for modeling interdependence and the associated repercussions for behavior. Social network analysis is more than a set of methods—it is an orientation towards the understanding of human behavior that focuses on the importance of social relations, as well as the set of tools that enable the investigation of social relations and their consequence. Social network analysis has numerous applications in criminology and criminal justice; it can facilitate understandings of peer influence, the structure of criminal organizations, and the contagion of social behavior. Perhaps most importantly, it can be a valuable tool used by practitioners for reducing crime.

References

Braga, A. A., D. M. Kennedy, E. J. Waring, and A. M. Piehl. 2001. Problem-oriented policing, deterrence, and youth violence: An evaluation of Boston's operation ceasefire. *Journal of Research in Crime and Delinquency* 38: 195-225.

Bunker, R. J., and J. P. Sullivan. 2001. Cartel evolution: Potentials and consequences. *Transnational Organized Crime* 4: 55-74.

Bursik, R. J. 1986. Delinquency rates as sources of ecological change. In J. M. Byrne and R. J. Sampson (Eds.), *The social ecology of crime* (pp. 63-74). New York: Springer-Verlag.

Bursik, R. J. 1988. Social disorganization and theories of crime and delinquency: Problems and prospects. *Criminology* 26: 519-551.

Burt, R. S. 1992. *Structural holes: The social structure of competition.* Cambridge, MA: Harvard University Press.

Carrington, P., J. Scott, and S. Wasserman. 2005. *Models and methods in social network analysis.* New York: Cambridge University Press.

Cartwright, D. S., K. I. Howard, and N. A. Reuterman. 1970. Multivariate analysis of gang delinquency, Part 2—Structural and dynamic properties of gangs. *Multivariate Behavioral Research* 5: 303-323.

Cloward, R. A., and L. E. Ohlin. 1960. *Delinquency and opportunity: A theory of delinquent gangs*. New York: Free Press.

Coady, W. F. 1985. Automated link analysis: Artificial intelligence-based tool for investigators. *Police Chief* 52: 22-23.

Cohen, A. K. 1955. *Delinquent boys: The culture of the gang*. New York: Free Press.

Coles, N. 2001. It's not what you know: It's who you know that counts. Analyzing serious crime groups as social networks. *The British Journal of Criminology* 41: 580-594.

Curry, G. D., and Decker, S. H. 2003. *Confronting gangs: Crime and community* (2nd ed.). Los Angeles, CA: Roxbury.

Davern, M., and D. S. Hachen. 2006. The role of information and influence in social networks: Examining the association between social network structure and job mobility. *American Journal of Economics and Sociology* 65: 269-293.

Davis, R. H. 1981. Social network analysis: An aid in conspiracy investigations. *FBI Law Enforcement Bulletin* 50: 11-19.

Decker, S. H. 1996. Collective and normative features of gang violence. *Justice Quarterly* 13: 243-264.

Decker, S. H. 2001. The impact of organizational features on gang activities and relationships. In M. W. Klein, H.-J. Kerner, C. L. Maxson, and E. G. M. Weitekamp (Eds.), *The Eurogang paradox: Street gangs and youth groups in the U.S. and Europe* (pp. 21-40). Dordrecht: Kluwer Academic.

Decker, S. H., and B. Van Winkle. 1994. Slinging dope: The role of gangs and gang members in drug sales. *Justice Quarterly* 11: 583-604.

Decker, S. H., and B. Van Winkle. 1996. *Life in the gang: Family, friends, and violence*. Cambridge: Cambridge University Press.

Finckenauer, J. O., and E. J. Waring. 1998. *Russian mafia in America: Immigration, culture, and crime*. Boston, MA: Northeastern University Press.

Fleisher, M. S. 2002. *Women and gangs: A field research study*. Washington, DC: Department of Justice, Office of Juvenile Justice and Delinquency Prevention.

Granovetter, M. 1973. The strength of weak ties. *American Journal of Sociology* 81: 1287-1303.

Haynie, D. L. 2001. Delinquent peers revisited: does network structure matter? *American Journal of Sociology* 106: 1013-1057.

Hirschi, T. 1969. *Causes of delinquency*. Berkeley, CA: University of California Press.

Howlett, J. B. 1980. Analytical investigative techniques: Tools for complex criminal investigations. *Police Chief* 47: 42-45.

Kennedy, D. M., A. A. Braga, and A. M. Piehl. 1997. The (un)known universe: Mapping gangs and gang violence in Boston. In D. Weisburd and T. McEwen (Eds.), *Crime mapping and crime prevention* (pp. 219-262). Monsey, NY: Criminal Justice Press.

Kennedy, D. M., A. A. Braga, A. M. Piehl, and E. J. Waring. 2001. *Reducing gun violence: The Boston Gun Project's Operation Ceasefire*. Washington, DC: National Institute of Justice.

Klein, M. W. 1995. *The American Street Gang: Its nature, prevalence, and control*. New York: Oxford University Press.

Klein, M. W. 1971. *Street gangs and street workers*. Englewood Cliffs, NJ: Prentice-Hall.

Klein, M. W., and C. L Maxson. 1994. Gangs and cocaine trafficking. In D. McKenzie and C. Uchida (Eds.), *Drugs and crime: Evaluating public policy initiatives* (pp. 42-58). Thousand Oaks, CA: Sage.

Klein, M. W., C. L. Maxson, and L. C. Cunningham. 1991. Crack, street gangs, and violence. *Criminology* 29: 623-650.

Krohn, M. D. 1986. The web of conformity: A network approach to the explanation of delinquent behavior. *Social Problems* 33: 81-93.

Lin, N. 1982. Social resources and instrumental action. In P. Marsden and N. Lin (Eds.), *Social structure and network analysis* (pp. 247-271). Beverly Hills, CA: Sage.

Lin, N. 1990. Social resources and social mobility: A structural theory of status attainment. In R. L. Breiger (Ed.), *Social mobility and social structure*. New York: Cambridge University Press.

Maltz, M. D. 1998. Visualizing homicide: A research note. *Journal of Quantitative Criminology* 14: 397-410.

McGloin, J. M. 2005a. Policy and intervention considerations of a network analysis of street gangs. *Criminology and Public Policy* 43: 607-636.

McGloin, J. M. 2005b. *Street gangs and interventions: Innovative problem solving with network analysis*. Washington, DC: US Department of Justice, Office of Community Oriented Policing.

McGloin, J. M., and A. R. Piquero. 2010. On the relationship between co-offending network redundancy and offending versatility. *Journal of Research in Crime and Delinquency* 47: 63-90.

McGloin, J. M., and L. O. Shermer. 2009. Self-control and deviant peer structure. *Journal of Research in Crime and Delinquency* 46: 35-72.

McIllwain, J. S. 1999. Organized crime: A social network approach. *Crime Law and Social Change* 32: 301-323.

Moreno, J. L. 1934. *Who shall survive?* New York: Beacon Press.

Morselli, C., and P. Tremblay. 2004. Criminal achievement, offender networks and the benefits of low self-control. *Criminology* 42: 773-804.

Natarajan, M. 2000. Understanding the structure of a drug trafficking organization: A conversational analysis. In M. Natarajan and M. Hough (Eds.), *Illegal drug markets: From research to prevention policy*. Monsey, NY: Criminal Justice Press/Willow Tree Press.

Natarajan, M. 2006. Understanding the structure of a large heroin distribution network: A quantitative analysis of qualitative data. *Journal of Quantitative Criminology* 22: 171-192.

Osgood, D. W., J. K. Wilson, and P. M. O'Malley. 1996. Routine activities and individual deviant behavior. *American Sociological Review* 5: 635-655.

Padilla, F. M. 1992. *The gang as an American enterprise*. New Brunswick, NJ: Rutgers University Press.

Papachristos, A. V. 2009. Murder by structure: Dominance relations and the social structure of gang homicide in Chicago. *American Journal of Sociology* 115: 74-128.

Peterson, D., J. Miller, and F. A. Esbensen. 2001. The impact of sex composition on gangs and gang member delinquency. *Criminology* 39: 411-440.

Podolny, J. M., and J Baron. 1997. Resources and relationships: Social networks and mobility in the workplace. *American Sociological Review* 62: 673-693.

Sampson, R. J., and W. B. Groves. 1989. Community structure and crime: Testing social disorganization theory. *American Journal of Sociology* 94: 744-802.

Sampson, R. J., S. W. Raudenbush, and F. Earls. 1997. Neighborhood and violent crime: A multilevel study of collective efficacy. *Science* 227: 918-924.

Sanchez-Jankowski, M. 1991. *Islands in the street: Gangs and American urban society*. Berkeley, CA: University of California Press.

Sarnecki, J. 2001. *Delinquent networks*. Cambridge: Cambridge University Press.

Schreck, C., J. M. McGloin, and D. Kirk. 2009. A study of the contrast between violent and nonviolent neighborhood crime rates in Chicago: What factors make for a violent neighborhood? *Justice Quarterly* 26: 771-794.

Scott, J. 2000. *Social network analysis: A handbook* (2nd ed.). London: Sage.

Shaw, C. R., and H. McKay. [1942]1969. *Juvenile delinquency and urban areas*. Chicago, IL: University of Chicago Press.

Short, J. F., and F. L. Strodtbeck. 1965. *Group process and gang delinquency*. Chicago, IL: University of Chicago.

Skolnick, J. T., T. Correl, E. Navarro, and R. Rabb. 1988. *The social structure of street drug dealing*. Sacramento, CA: Office of the Attorney General of the State of California.

Smith, S. S. 2005. "Don't put my name on it": Social capital activation and job-finding assistance among the black urban poor. *American Journal of Sociology* 111: 1-57.

Stelfox, P. 1996. *Gang violence: Strategic and tactical options*. Manchester: Crown Copyright.

Sutherland, E. H. 1947. *Principles of criminology* (4th ed.). Philadelphia, PA: J.B. Lippincott.

Taylor, C. 1990. *Dangerous society*. East Lansing, MI: Michigan State University Press.

Tita, G., J. K. Riley, and P. Greenwood. 2005. *Reducing gun violence: Operation ceasefire in Los Angeles, research in brief*. Washington, DC: National Institute of Justice.

Warr, M. 2002. *Companions in crime: The social aspects of criminal conduct*. Cambridge: Cambridge University Press.

Wasserman, S., and K. Faust. 1994. *Social network analysis: Methods and applications*. Cambridge: Cambridge University Press.

Weisel, D. L. 1999. *Persistence and rising prevalence of contemporary gangs: An organizational analysis*. Ann Arbor, MI: Dissertation Services.

Yablonsky, L. 1962. *The violent gang*. New York: Macmillan.

A User-Friendly Introduction to Panel Data Modeling

John L. Worrall

This paper offers a brief user-friendly introduction to panel data modeling in criminal justice and criminology. The author assumes that the reader is familiar with ordinary least squares regression. Topics covered include the problems of pooling data over time and space, model selection, and estimation issues in a fixed-effects context. The paper concludes with a look at some extensions that help researchers model and/or account for simultaneity, heterogeneous year effects, unit-specific effects, and events.

Ordinary least squares regression is not equipped to deal with repeated observations on the same units of analysis. Problems arise when researchers pool their data across both time and space. One solution to such problems is the estimation of panel data models. "Panel data" refer, simply, to observations on same units (e.g., individuals, organizations, cities, states) collected at multiple points in time. Most panel data are compiled in yearly increments (see, e.g., Evans and Owens 2007; Marvell and Moody 1996; Zhao, Scheider, and Thurman 2002), which is likely due to availability, but there is no requirement that data should be observed in yearly increments.

It would be convenient if statisticians and econometricians used the same terminology across disciplines, especially in the panel data context. In political science, researchers often refer to "time series-cross section" (TSCS) models. In other disciplines, and even in criminology and criminal justice, "multiple time series" (MTS) refers to multiple observations on the same units. Some have argued that TSCS data contain many observations on relatively few units (Beck and Katz 1995); yet, researchers have used the language of TSCS—and MTS—when analyzing data that could just as easily be described as being of the panel variety (e.g., Kovandzic and Sloan 2002). No matter the choice of terminology, many of the same issues arise when the sample consists of the same units observed over more than one time period (Kristensen and Wawro 2003).

Despite the problems of pooling (discussed in detail shortly), there are significant advantages to it. By collecting data on the same units over time, researchers can increase their sample sizes by increasing the number of time periods. This makes it feasible, for example, to conduct state-level analysis. That there are 50 states makes statistical estimation practically impossible, but if, say, 10 years of data are collected, that sample of 50 increases to 500. Not only does the sample size increase but also researchers are afforded an opportunity to control for unobserved (and, perhaps, inconceivable) time-stable factors associated with each unit of analysis. In county-level research, for example, a case can easily be made that county A is fundamentally different from county B. Panel data models permit researchers to effectively control for such differences.

The Problems

Three problems arise when data are pooled over time and space. In the typical cross-sectional dataset, statistical estimation does not raise autocorrelation (or serial dependence) concerns. Indeed, autocorrelation is impossible if data are collected at one point in time. In the panel data context, however, because a time dimension is included, researchers are all but forced to address the possibility that data in time period A are correlated with data in time period B. This is normal and expected, especially in research on aggregate units. Large cities, for example, tend to stay large over a long period of time. The same holds at the individual-level. We know that people exhibit characteristics that are relatively constant over time. A tall adult stays relatively tall throughout his or her lifespan.

Ordinary least squares assumes that errors are homoskedastic, that is, constant across units. When this assumption is not met, the result, of course, is heteroskedasticity. When heteroskedasticity is present, researchers need to take steps to control for it. But when data are pooled across space *and* time, heteroskedasticity problems, if they exist, become compounded. When a time dimension is added to the data, the effects of heteroskedasticity increase in accordance with the number of time periods in the data (Stimson 1985, p. 919). The more time periods there are, the more problems heteroskedasticity can pose.

The third problem that arises in the panel data context is heterogeneity. This occurs when all units are affected by a "shock" during the same time period. In a state-level panel data analysis, an example of one such shock could be a presidential election. As a presidential election would affect all states to some extent, the errors across each state will be correlated due to the event each experienced. Such a tendency would be largely undetectable in a cross-sectional dataset. So, while panel data are advantageous from a sample size and "control" standpoint, there are clearly some issues that need to be addressed.

Model Selection

At the risk of simplification, there are two main choices for panel data modeling: fixed effects estimation and random effects estimation. There are *many* other modeling choices, and new models for panel data modeling continue to be developed, but most bear a fair degree of resemblance to these two main techniques. What is the difference between these? In order to answer this question, let us first consider the basic cross-sectional ordinary least squares (OLS) model. In matrix notation, it is:

$$y = \alpha + \beta x + \varepsilon \tag{1}$$

The variable y in Equation 1 is, of course, the dependent variable, variable α is the intercept, variable x is a vector of independent variables, variable β represents the regression coefficients, and variable ε is the error term. When the data are pooled over time and space, Equation 1 extends to something like this:

$$y_{i,t} = \alpha + \beta x_{i,t} + \varepsilon_{i,t} \tag{2}$$

Note the addition of the i and t subscripts in Equation 2. These denote units and time periods, respectively. Also, note that there is nothing different between Equations 1 and 2, other than the fact that Equation 2 shows that there are repeated observations on the same units. Finally, although Equation 2 is not a model that we want to estimate, it is sometimes called the "constant coefficients model." It assumes that the regression coefficients are constant across units and time periods. In fact, Equation 2 makes no attempt to explicitly model the repeated observations. Fixed effects and random effects models do just this and address some of the problems associated with estimating the constant coefficients model via OLS.

The fixed effects model, again in matrix notation, looks like this:

$$y_{i,t} = \alpha_i + \delta_t + \beta x_{i,t} + \varepsilon_{i,t} \tag{3}$$

Note that Equation 3 is basically the same as Equation 2, with several key exceptions. First, Equation 3 adds separate intercepts for each unit. This is denoted by α_i. Second, it adds δ_t, which denotes a dummy variable for each time period. We will look later at the logic for adding these unit and time dummies. For now, though, contrast Equation 3 with the random effects model, which typically looks like this:

$$y_{i,t} = \alpha + \beta x_{i,t} + u_i + w_t + \varepsilon_{i,t} \tag{4}$$

Also called an "error components model," Equation 4 is different from Equation 3 in that Equation 4 adds u_i and w_t, each of which denotes a separate error term, the former for the units analyzed and the latter for the time periods. Equation 4 assumes that the unobserved differences between units and time periods are random variables. In contrast, the fixed effects model assumes that they are fixed. In one sense, it is easier to wrap one's head around Equation 3 because the unit and time period effects are modeled explicitly.

Choosing between Random and Fixed Effects Models

What considerations go into choosing between the random and fixed effects models? There are three of them: (1) the size of N and T; (2) whether there is correlation between the error term and the unobserved variables; and (3) whether predictors vary over time. For those who do not feel comfortable in choosing between either approach on the basis of these considerations, there is a test that helps researchers decide between one approach and the other. It will be considered, too. First, though, let us look at each of the three main considerations in more depth.

Size of N and T

Fixed effects estimation in large samples can be unwieldy and sacrifice precious degrees of freedom. Consider a sample of 1000 cities observed in yearly increments for a full decade. To model the α_i in Equation 3, the researcher would need to add 999 additional parameters to the model, and this is just to model the city effects. Some are not comfortable in sacrificing degrees of freedom in this fashion and, as such, opt for random effects estimation.

Related to the problem of unwieldy models is the problem of complicated interpretation. The coefficients for the unit and time dummies are themselves rarely interesting from an interpretation standpoint, but for those who are interested, making sense of the relationships can be complicated. And there is another concern:

> [Fixed effects estimation...] removes any of the average unit-to-unit variation from the analysis. The introduction of fixed effects for each unit, for example, simply asks whether intraunit changes in some dependent variable are associated with intraunit changes in one or more independent variables. In other words, fixed effects estimation ignores the possibility that unit-to-unit variation sheds light on the relationship between x and y. (Worrall 2008a, p. 235)

Correlation between the Error Term and Unobserved Variables

Random effects estimation is more efficient, which would seem to make it a logical choice. However, a key assumption underlying the random effects approach is zero correlation between the error term and predictor variables. More specifically, the predictor variables should be correlated with the unobserved unit-specific error terms (the u_i in Equation 4).

A related assumption underlying the random effects approach is that the errors are constant across time (see the w_t in Equation 4). This assumption is difficult to meet in most real-world situations (Berk 2004, pp. 178-180). Why, for example, would some unmeasured event have a constant effect across all time periods observed?

Time Invariant Predictors

In choosing between random and fixed effects estimation, it is also important to consider whether predictor variables vary over time. If a predictor does not vary over time, it will be perfectly collinear with the unit dummies in a fixed effects setting. As an example of such a problematic predictor, one may wish to denote whether a particular jurisdiction is conservative or liberal with a "1" or a "0." This approach should always be avoided in fixed effects estimation.

In a similar vein, if one wishes to estimate the effect of an event that affected every unit at the same point in time (say, e.g., the 9/11 terrorist attacks), then such a variable will be perfectly collinear with time dummy variables (Allison 1994). It is still possible, in some situations, to estimate the effects of events in a fixed effects context, but we will turn attention to that later.

Finally, predictors that change slowly over time are also problematic. As Beck (2001, p. 285) observed, "Although we can estimate [a model] with slowly changing independent variables, the fixed effect will soak up most of the explanatory power of these slowly changing variables. Thus, if a variable ... changes over time, but slowly, the fixed effects will make it hard for such variables to appear either substantively or statistically significant." Plumper and Troeger (2007) pioneered a fixed effects vector composition procedure to deal with this, so it is a problem that can be overcome (see Worrall 2008b, for an application).

The Hausman Test

There is also a statistical test for choosing between random and fixed effects estimation: the so-called Hausman test (Hausman 1978). It is a test of the null hypothesis that random effects would be consistent and efficient against the alternative hypothesis that random effects would be inconsistent. The key question underlying the test is whether there is significant correlation between the unobserved unit-specific random effects and the predictors. If there is no correlation, then it may be desirable to opt for the random effects approach.

The test statistic is as follows: $[(\beta_{FE} - \beta_{RE})/(s^2{}_{\beta FE} - s^2{}_{\beta RE})]$. The β_{FE} are the fixed effects model coefficients, the β_{RE} are the random effects model coefficients, and the $s^2{}_{\beta FE}$ and $s^2{}_{\beta RE}$ are the variances of the fixed and random effects model coefficients, respectively. The Hausman statistic has a chi-square distribution with as many degrees of freedom as there are predictors in the model. If the *p*-value is insignificant (i.e., greater than 0.05), this means it is probably safe to use random effects estimation. Fixed effects should be used, however, if the statistic is significant. The Hausman test offers somewhat an objective take on whether one should use random or fixed effects estimation. Yet, researchers should not put total faith in it. They should also consider the issues discussed in the preceding subsections.

Estimation Issues

In the interest of keeping it simple, the remainder of this paper will be limited to fixed effects modeling. Also, it is this author's observation that criminologists and criminal justice researchers tend to opt more frequently for fixed rather than random effects estimation (see, e.g., Worrall 2008b, p. 789). Finally, it is also worth focusing on fixed effects because of how unlikely it is for the random effects error terms to be uncorrelated with the model's predictors.

A researcher's work is by no means done once he or she selects fixed in lieu of random effects estimation. There are at least five key estimation issues that deserve consideration. They are: (1) heterogeneity; (2) dynamics; (3) panel heteroskedasticity; (4) stationarity; and (5) trends. More often than not, several of these issues present themselves in the same research context. Moreover, this list is partial and certainly does not cover *all* problems that a researcher could encounter.

Heterogeneity

In the panel data context, "heterogeneity" refers to differences in the units of analysis. If a researcher has a panel dataset on, say, 1,000 cities, all of different sizes, then common sense suggests that most, if not all, of the cities will differ from one another in key respects. Cherry (1999) offers this illustration:

> "Suppose there are two criminal justice departments. Department A follows strict accounting practices that report high percentages of crimes, while department B is more lenient and reports lower percentages. Noting that certainty of sanctions is typically measured by the clearance rate, this disparity causes a problem when the reported data from the two jurisdictions are analyzed. (p. 754)

The same issue presents itself in a cross-sectional context, but researchers, not having access to data collected across some span of time, cannot do much about it. With the use of unit-specific dummy variables in a fixed effects context, however, researchers can control for unobserved differences between each city. They can do the same with time periods. If data are collected in yearly increments, then it is common to include year dummies to capture time effects.

Why not just enter year and unit dummies as a default condition? Degrees of freedom are lost with either approach, so it may prove helpful to test whether unit and/or year dummies are even needed. One common approach, particularly in terms of unit dummies, which tend to gobble up many degrees of freedom, is to conduct a simple *F*-test. If the *F*-test for all the unit dummies is significant, they should be modeled. It bears mentioning, though, that it is not difficult to achieve significance with such a test. It may be less likely to obtain a significant statistic when conducting an *F*-test on the year dummies.

Researchers often *assume* that both unit and year dummies are necessary in fixed effects estimation. More often than not, it is advisable that they should be included. However, researchers should do their homework and make sure that either of them is necessary.

Dynamics

A more pressing issue in the panel data context, and particularly in terms of fixed effects estimation, is that of dynamics. Panel data are rarely independent across the time dimension, as one unit's value during the current time period is probably quite correlated with its value on the same variable in a previous time period (Hanushek and Jacson 1977; Maddala 1992). Worrall and Pratt (2004 offered this example:

> It is commonly understood that when public agencies do not spend their budgetary allotments for a particular year, their budgets can be reduced in subsequent years. Thus, the very nature of the public budgeting process ensures that an agency's budget for one year is highly associated with its budget for the previous year. (p. 89)

There are several approaches for detecting serial correlation in panel data, but one straightforward approach is to take the following steps: (1) estimate an OLS regression model; (2) regress the residuals on all of the independent variables and the lagged residual; and (3) check whether the coefficient on the lagged residual is significant. If the coefficient is significant, it is safe to conclude that serial correlation is present.

Assuming that there is autocorrelation in the data, what can be done? One approach is, simply, to include one or more lags of the dependent variable in the main model. This is an attractive approach when there are more time periods than units (Beck and Katz 1995). A number of criminologists have included lagged dependent variables in their panel data models, however, without much attention the number of units compared with the number of time periods (e.g., Kovandzic, Sloan, and Vieraitis 2002; Lilley and Boba 2008; Marvell and Moody 1996). When there are more units than time periods and researchers lag the dependent variable to control for autocorrelation, this can result in "Nickel bias" (Nickel 1981), which, in a short time series, can push coefficients toward zero.

Lagging the dependent variable also suffers from two additional problems. One is that it results in lost observations (i.e., it is not possible to lag the dependent variable in the first time period). Another more important problem is that lagging the dependent variable makes for a dynamic model. It then becomes necessary to make it clear that the results are "short-run" estimates. Adjustments to the standard errors must be made in order to arrive at long-run estimates (e.g., De Boef and Keele 2008).

Another approach to dealing with serial correlation is to estimate models that include first-order autoregressive disturbance terms. This is done by estimating

ρ from β in a residual regression of $u_{it} = \beta u_{i,t-1} + \eta_{it}$ (Hsiao 1986; Mundlak 1978). Most statistics packages allow for such estimation (e.g., Stata's-xtregar-command).

Still, other approaches for dealing with autocorrelation include estimation models with robust standard errors (e.g., by using Stata's-robust-feature) or estimating models that are robust to autocorrelation, especially if the form is unknown. The generalized method of moments is considered robust to autocorrelation of unknown form (for an overview, see Wooldridge 2001).

Panel Heteroskedasticity and Contemporaneous Correlation

In their seminal work, Beck and Katz (1995) highlight the problems associated with panel heteroskedasticity and contemporaneous correlation. The former is concerned with unit-to-unit variances in the errors. Franzese (2002) proposed a simple test for detecting this problem. It entails regressing the absolute values of the OLS residuals on the unit-specific dummy variables. A resulting significant *F*-test suggests the presence of panel heteroskedasticity. Very few criminologists and/or criminal justice researchers have made any effort to detect or correct for this problem.

Contemporaneous correlation is concerned with correlated errors between two or more units at the same time. This is different from the heterogeneity discussed earlier, as it is conceivable that an event affects a few (though not all) of the units at the same time. Tests for detecting contemporaneous correlation are particularly intuitive, so motivated readers may wish to explore the work of Breusch and Pagan (1980). Otherwise, for those who use Stata, the user-written—xttest2—may prove helpful.

Nonstationarity

Panel data must be stationary, meaning that the means, variances, and auto-covariances (at various lags) stay constant across time periods. The augmented Dickey-Fuller test can be used to test for nonstationarity. This test involves regressing the first-differenced dependent variable on the one-period lag of the dependent variable as well as lags of the first-differenced dependent variables (Enders 1995). A number of different, more sophisticated tests have been introduced in the recent years (e.g., Choi 2001; Hadri 2000; Im, Pesaran, and Shin 2003). Stata users now have access to the—xtunitroot—command to check whether panels are stationary. The assorted tests accommodate balanced as well as unbalanced panels, the latter being panels with either more time periods than units or more units than time periods. For more on dealing with nonstationarity, see Banerjee (1999).

Pre-existing Trends

The inclusion of unit- and time-specific dummies in a fixed effects context, while advantageous for reasons touched on earlier, simplifies reality. Some researchers have built on this approach by replacing the unit dummies with unit-specific trend variables, typically coded with a 1 to T for each unit. If a panel contains 10 years of data, then each unit would get its own variable coded 1 through 10 for each time period. Such trend variables help control for trends in each unit that depart from *annual* events captured by the time dummies (Black and Nagin 1998; Marvell and Moody 1996). Whether this approach is desirable or necessary hinges on several factors, including the data in question and the substantive question at hand.

Extensions

Continuing with our focus on fixed effects estimation, there are several extensions that researchers may wish to consider. The ones that we will consider here help researchers model and/or account for: (1) simultaneity; (2) heterogeneous year effects; (3) unit-specific effects; and (4) events. These extensions not only add a level of sophistication to any one study, but they also make it more feasible for researchers to deal with real-world problems.

Simultaneity

A number of panel data studies published in criminology and criminal justice journals have examined the effects on aggregate crime rates of various policies. For example, many have studied the effect of policing on crime rates (e.g., Marvell and Moody 1996; Worrall and Kovandzic 2007). Others have sought to determine whether state laws, such as three-strikes, affect crime rates at various levels (e.g., Kovandzic, Sloan, and Vieraitis 2004). A problem arises in both situations. While the policies in question may affect crime, crime most likely affects the policies. For example, state legislatures do not enact three-strikes laws in a vacuum. Concerns over crime are at least partially responsible for their passage. Researchers, then, need to account for this problem. For ease of exposition, we will call it the "simultaneity problem."

One solution to deal with the simultaneity problem—that works in both a cross-sectional and panel data context—is to estimate instrumental variables regressions. Briefly, this involves identifying a variable that is correlated with a problematic predictor (the one that is thought to be affected by the dependent variable) and that is uncorrelated with the error term in the main equation. At the risk of simplification, this new variable (the instrument) basically replaces the problematic predictor. A common problematic predictor in the literature is police presence, or "police levels," usually measured as officers per capita.

Researchers have identified a number of creative instruments for police levels, ranging from federal grants to (e.g., Evans and Owens 2007; Government Accountability Office 2005), mayoral elections (Levitt 1997) and firefighters hired (Levitt 2002).

Researchers who opt for the instrumental variables approach to dealing with simultaneity in their panel data models need to be cognizant of the so-called "local average treatment effects" (e.g., Angrist and Imbens 1995; Heckman, Urzua, and Vytlacil 2006; Heckman and Vytlacil 2005). Basically, a problematic predictor (in the above example, police levels) is affected by multiple factors, not just by the instruments selected. So, the findings will be "local" to the selected instruments.

Panel data also afford researchers with another technique to address the simultaneity problem, namely, the Granger causality test (Granger 1969; Pindyck and Rubinfeld 1991, pp. 216-219). The test, which involves two separate autoregressive analyses, has been used on a few occasions in criminology (e.g., Kovandzic et al. 2002; Marvell and Moody 1996). Consider, again, an analysis of the effect of police levels on crime. The first step is to regress crime on lags of itself and lags of police levels (and the controls). The number of lags on each depends on how many are significant. The first lags that become insignificant are dropped. If, after the proper number of lags has been selected, lags of police levels are significant, it is said that police levels "Granger cause" crime. The second test is similar, but in it, police levels serve as the dependent variable. Then lags of it and lags of crime (along with controls) appear on the right-hand side of the equation. If lagged crime is significant, then it "Granger cause" police. There are two problems with this approach, however. One is that observations are lost. Another is that the use of lags means it is impossible to determine whether policing affects crime or crime affects police in the current time period.

Heterogeneous Year Effects

Using panel data, Worrall (2008c) found that the Local Law Enforcement Block Grants led to significant reductions in serious crime. There were two possible problems with this finding. First, police forces may have already been expanding beforehand, making the relationship between grants and crime spurious. Second, crime may have already been on the decline, a trend that would not have been captured in the models. In response to this problem, Worrall (2008c) emulated an approach taken by the Government Accountability Office (2005) and Evans and Owens (2007) wherein heterogeneous year effects were calculated and then used to replace the year dummies. Worrall (2008c) described the procedure thusly:

> These effects were calculated by (1) regressing police levels in the pre-LLEBG period on a linear time trend for each unit; (2) doing the same for the aggregate crime rate; (3) organizing the coefficients from each regression into quartiles; and (4) interacting the resulting cells with year dummies. (p. 343)

Because there were 12 years of data in his analysis, this resulted in 192 separate year effects (four quartiles from the first regression × four quartiles from the second regression × 12 years of data). For more details on this procedure, see Evans and Owens (2007, p. 192) and Government Accountability Office (2005, p. 77).

Unit-Specific Effects

Black and Nagin (1998, p. 213) called attention to what they termed as a "geographic aggregation assumption," or the assumption that parameters are constant across all units analyzed. Reality, unfortunately, is rarely this simple. The typical panel data model of, say, the effect of a new law on crime will yield a single coefficient for the law variable. But it is naive to assume that the law would work in the same way in all areas examined. Indeed, Pesaran and Smith (1995) found that this can result in significant bias. What, then, can be done? Black and Nagin (1998) adopted the simple approach of interacting the unit dummies with the predictor variable of interest. In their case, the key predictor was a "right to carry" (RTC) variable (coded with 1 or 0 to denote the presence or absence of a RTC law in any given state).

Black and Nagin's (1998) work was important, as it resulted in one of the first major attacks on Lott and Mustard's (1997) controversial finding that RTC laws were inversely associated with crime. Needless to say, gun control advocates were not impressed with the findings. And, when Black and Nagin estimated unit-specific (or, in their case, state-specific) effects, they concluded:

> We strongly reject the Lott and Mustard model's assumption of a uniform impact across states ... The estimates are disparate. Murders decline in Florida but increase in West Virginia. Assaults fall in Maine but increase in Pennsylvania. (pp. 213-214)

Modeling the Effects of Events

Campbell and Stanley (1967, pp. 55-57) went so far as to call panel designs as "excellent quasi-experimental design[s], perhaps the best of the more feasible designs." Their observation rings true, in part, because panel data lend themselves nicely to the study of events. When some units experience an event and others do not, it is akin to having treatment and control conditions in a classical experiment (minus the random assignment, of course). Panel designs have proven quite popular of late in criminology and criminal justice, particularly for their ability to model events.

An "event" can take on many manifestations, but, generally, the term refers to some "happening" or condition that affects all or several units and one or many points in time. In models of aggregate crime rates, the event is most often a policy change or a law. There are multiple options available for the modeling of each, but four approaches have proven quite popular for modeling events in a panel data context (see Allison 1994, for an overview).

The first and most basic approach is to create a 1,0 variable denoting the presence or absence of the event or condition. This approach is quite popular for examining the effects of state laws on state crime rates. The state law variable is coded with a "1" for those states that have the law in question, or "0" otherwise. But researchers need to be careful with this approach because if the event or condition affects all units at the same time, then the resulting variable will be perfectly collinear with time dummies (see earlier discussion on "Choosing between Random and Fixed Effects").

The 1,0 variable approach is limited in that it fails to reveal any details about the event/condition in question. It may also be impossible in a fixed effects context for reasons just mentioned. An alternative is to code the event/condition in levels—if the data are available. For example, in studies of the effect on crime of policing grants (e.g., Worrall and Kovandzic 2007; Zhao et al. 2002), this approach is quite feasible. The crude 1,0 variable is replaced with the value of the grant secured (usually the amount is divided by population and multiplied by some metric). If a jurisdiction does not get a grant, it gets coded with a "0." The advantage of this coding strategy, aside from overcoming the collinearity problem highlighted in the previous paragraph, is that it reveals additional details about what crime returns can be expected with each additional dollar of spending.

Researchers have also opted to measure events and conditions with trend variables. Although somewhat crude, this approach is at least creative. An example of it appears in Marvell and Moody's (2001) study of the "lethal effects" of three-strikes laws. They sought to measure the incapacitative effect of three-strikes laws, with a linear trend variable starting at the time when the law was enacted. In their words, the variable "assumes that, in the absence of the law, very few defendants would have escaped prison sentences, so the incapacitation effect grows over time" (p. 103). Researchers have had a difficult time separating deterrent from incapacitative effects, so Marvell and Moody deserve a certain measure of credit for trying (see also Kessler and Levitt 1999).

Linear time trends, 1,0 variables, and even coding events and conditions in levels may simplify reality. It is not a stretch to conceive of nonlinear effects. For example, funding may be helpful to a certain amount and then yields fewer returns as amounts increase. Alternatively, a law may reduce crime in the short term and then have little effect some years later. Various linear and nonlinear coding schemes are possible to address these and related complications. Readers would be well advised to consult Allison (1994) for a thorough treatment of the alternative coding schemes.

Conclusion

This paper has provided a brief and simple introduction to panel data modeling. The author has assumed throughout that the reader is familiar with OLS regression. For those who have yet to attempt panel data modeling, there are many additional—and more thorough—introductions to the technique that they may wish to consult (see, e.g., Baltagi 2008; Hsiao 1986; Wooldridge 2002). Otherwise, it is recommended, to recap, that researchers follow this process:

(1) Choose between random and fixed effects estimation on the basis of three considerations: (i) the size of N relative to T; (ii) whether there is a correlation between the error term and the unobserved variables; and (iii) whether the predictors vary over time. A Hausman test is also recommended.
(2) Model heterogeneity only if necessary.
(3) Be cognizant of dynamics and panel heteroskedasticity.
(4) Test for stationarity.
(5) Consider modeling pre-existing trends, if they are present.

Once these steps are taken, researchers can then venture into more sophisticated territory by correcting for simultaneity, if present, accounting for heterogeneous year effects, modeling unit-specific effects, and examining the effects of events. This author is partial to the fixed effects, once again, because of its frequent use in criminology and criminal justice—and also because many of the extensions introduced toward the latter part of this paper would not be possible in a random effects context.

References

Allison, P. D. 1994. Using panel data to estimate the effects of events. *Sociological Methods and Research* 23: 174-199.

Angrist, J. D., and G. W. Imbens. 1995. Two-stage least squares estimation of average causal effects in models with variable treatment intensity. *Journal of the American Statistical Association* 90: 431-442.

Baltagi, B. 2008. *Econometric analysis of panel data* (4th ed.). San Francisco, CA: Wiley.

Banerjee, A. 1999. Panel data unit roots and cointegration: An overview. *Oxford Bulletin of Economics and Statistics* 61: 607-629.

Beck, N. 2001. Time-series—Cross-section data: What have we learned in the past few years? *Annual Review of Political Science* 4: 271-293.

Beck, N., and J. N. Katz. 1995. What to do (and not to do) with time-series cross-section data. *American Political Science Review* 89: 634-674.

Berk, R. A. 2004. *Regression analysis: A constructive critique*. Thousand Oaks, CA: Sage.

Black, D. A., and D. S. Nagin. 1998. Do right-to-carry laws deter violent crime? *Journal of Legal Studies* 27: 209-219.

Breusch, T., and A. Pagan. 1980. The LM test and its applications to model specification in econometrics. *Review of Economic Studies* 47: 239-254.

Campbell, D. T., and J. C. Stanley. 1967. *Experimental and quasi-experimental designs for research*. Chicago: Rand McNally.

Cherry, T. L. 1999. Unobserved heterogeneity bias when estimating the economic model of crime. *Applied Economics Letters* 6: 753-757.

Choi, I. 2001. Unit root tests for panel data. *Journal of International Money and Finance* 20: 249-272.

De Boef, S., and L. Keele. 2008. Taking time seriously: Dynamic regression. *American Journal of Political Science* 52: 184-200.

Enders, W. 1995. *Applied econometric time series*. New York: Wiley.

Evans, N., and E. Owens. 2007. COPS and crime. *Journal of Public Economics* 91: 181-201.

Franzese, R. J. 2002. *Macroeconomic policies of developed democracies*. Cambridge: Cambridge University Press.

Government Accountability Office. 2005. *Community policing grants: COPS Grants were a modest contributor to declines in crime in the 1990s*. Washington, DC: Government Accountability Office.

Granger, C. W. J. 1969. Investigating causal relations by econometric models and cross-spectral methods. *Econometrica* 37: 424-438.

Hadri, K. 2000. Testing for stationarity in heterogeneous panel data. *Econometrics Journal* 3: 148-161.

Hanushek, E. A., and J. E. Jackson. 1977. *Statistical modeling for social scientists*. San Diego, CA: Academic Press.

Hausman, J. A. 1978. Specification tests in econometrics. *Econometrica* 46: 1251-1271.

Heckman, J. J., S. Urzua, and E. Vytlacil. 2006. Understanding instrumental variables in models with essential heterogeneity. *Review of Economics and Statistics* 88: 389-432.

Heckman, J. D., and E. Vytlacil. 2005. Structural equations, treatment effects, and econometric policy evaluation. *Econometrica* 73: 669-738.

Hsiao, C. 1986. *Analysis of panel data*. New York: Cambridge University Press.

Im, K. S., M. H. Pesaran, and Y. Shin. 2003. Testing for unit roots in heterogeneous panels. *Journal of Econometrics* 115: 53-74.

Kessler, D., and S. D. Levitt. 1999. Using sentence enhancements to distinguish between deterrence and incapacitation. *Journal of Law and Economics* 42: 343-363.

Kovandzic, T. V., and J. J. Sloan. 2002. Police levels and crime rates revisited: A county-level analysis from Florida (1980-1998). *Journal of Criminal Justice* 30: 65-76.

Kovandzic, T. V., J. J. Sloan, and L. M. Vieraitis. 2002. Unintended consequences of politically popular sentencing policy: The homicide promoting effects of "three strikes" in U.S. Cities (1980-1999). *Criminology and Public Policy* 1: 399-424.

Kovandzic, T. V., J. J. Sloan, and L. M. Vieraitis. 2004. "Striking out" as crime reduction policy: The impact of "three strikes" laws on crime rates in U.S. cities. *Justice Quarterly* 21: 207-239.

Kristensen, I. P., and G. Wawro. 2003, July. *Lagging the dog? The robustness of panel corrected standard errors in the presence of serial correlation and observation specific effects*. Paper presented at the annual meeting of the Society for Political Methodology, University of Minnesota, Minneapolis, MN.

Levitt, S. D. 1997. Using electoral cycles in police hiring to estimate the effect of police on crime. *American Economic Review* 87: 270-290.

Levitt, S. D. 2002. Using electoral cycles in police hiring to estimate the effect of police on crime: Reply. *American Economic Review* 92: 1244-1250.

Lilley, D., and R. Boba. 2008. A comparison of outcomes associated with two key law enforcement grant programs. *Criminal Justice Policy Review* 19: 438-465.

Lott, J. R., and D. B. Mustard. 1997. Crime, deterrence, and right-to-carry concealed handguns. *Journal of Legal Studies* 26: 1-68.

Maddala, G. S. 1992. *Introduction to econometrics*. New York: Macmillan.

Marvell, T. B., and C. E. Moody. 1996. Specification problems, police levels, and crime rates. *Criminology* 34: 609-643.

Marvell, T. B., and C. E. Moody. 2001. The lethal effects of three-strikes laws. *Journal of Legal Studies* 30: 89-106.

Mundlak, Y. 1978. On the pooling of time series and cross section data. *Econometrica* 46: 69-85.

Nickel, S. 1981. Biases in dynamic models with fixed effects. *Econometrica* 49: 1417-1426.
Pesaran, M. H., and R. Smith. 1995. Estimating long-run relationships from dynamic heterogeneous panels. *Journal of Econometrics* 68: 79-113.
Pindyck, R. S., and D. L. Rubinfeld. 1991. *Econometric models and economic forecasts.* New York: McGraw-Hill.
Plumper, V., and V. E. Troeger. 2007. Efficient estimation of time-invariant and rarely changing variables in finite sample panel analyses with unit fixed effects. *Political Analysis* 15: 124-139.
Stimson, J. 1985. Regression in space and time: A statistical essay. *American Journal of Political Science* 29: 914-947.
Wooldridge, J. M. 2001. Applications of generalized method of moments estimation. *Journal of Economic Perspectives* 15: 87-100.
Wooldridge, J. M. 2002. *Econometric analysis of cross section and panel data.* Cambridge, MA: MIT Press.
Worrall, J. L. 2008a. An introduction to pooling cross-sectional and time series data. In S. Menard (Ed.), *Handbook of longitudinal research: Design, measurement, and analysis* (pp. 233-248). New York: Elsevier.
Worrall, J. L. 2008b. Racial composition, unemployment, and crime: Dealing with inconsistencies in panel designs. *Social Science Research* 37: 787-800.
Worrall, J. L. 2008c. The effects of local law enforcement block grants on serious crime. *Criminology and Public Policy* 7: 325-350.
Worrall, J. L., and T. V. Kovandzic. 2007. COPS grants and crime revisited. *Criminology* 45: 159-190.
Worrall, J. L., and T. C. Pratt. 2004. On the consequences of ignoring unobserved heterogeneity when estimating macro-level models of crime. *Social Science Research* 33: 79-105.
Zhao, J., M. C. Scheider, and Q. C. Thurman. 2002. Funding community policing to reduce crime: Have COPS grants made a difference? *Criminology and Public Policy* 2: 7-32.

Censored Regression in Response to the Distributional Realities of Crime and Justice Measures

Christopher J. Sullivan and Tara Livelsberger

Regression modeling is the predominant analytic approach utilized in crime and justice studies. In its standard form, however, this analytic approach makes demands of data that often are ill-suited to the realities of measuring criminal behavior and justice responses to it. Censored dependent variables that contain a strong "floor" or "ceiling" in their observed values represent one case in point. This paper considers the prevalence of such variables in crime and justice research, highlights the implications of the problem, and discusses some potential alternatives. In doing so, it presents examples from the extant literature to illustrate key principles. The discussion concludes by offering some practical guidelines for application and information on available software tools.

Introduction

While there continues to be discussion regarding the prevalence of opportunities to engage in crime (e.g., Gottfredson and Hirschi 2003; Hay and Forrest 2008; Tittle, Ward, and Grasmick 2003), opportunities to apply multiple regression in criminology and criminal justice research certainly appear to be ubiquitous. Multiple regression modeling is a dominant analytic method in this field and social science more generally. In fact, multiple regression instruction in criminology and criminal justice may even outstrip that of discussions of key research design and data collection topics (Sullivan and Maxfield 2003). The application of this set of analytic tools is equally extensive. For example, eight of the nine articles in the December 2009 issue of *Justice Quarterly* utilized multivariate regression methods in some fashion. That trend is repeated in other issues of the journal, and others in the field of criminology and criminal justice.

While it is important that a field has a shared analytic language from which various substantive questions can be studied, researchers must continually assess how particular analytic strategies shape information garnered on issues of interest. Given the extensive application of regression methods, and their associated limitations, it is important that analysis proceeds in a careful and reflective manner if we wish to obtain appropriate answers to relevant theoretical and policy questions (Berk 2004). One area of concern involves the fit between the dependent variable and the assumptions of the statistical model in which it is studied. "Criminologists have the unfortunate lot of studying a phenomenon that is inherently difficult to measure" (Osgood, McMorris, and Potenza 2002, p. 267) and, by extension, those studying crime and system response must overcome obstacles in analyzing these often recalcitrant variables.

This paper considers the "censored" dependent variables that are commonly observed in crime and justice research. They represent one category of measures, such as dichotomies and ordinal scales, which are limited and therefore may not be wholly appropriate for standard regression modeling (Long 1997). The paper begins by defining the condition at the center of the discussion and considers its prevalence and scope in crime and justice research. We then examine the problems inherent in applying standard modeling approaches to such variables and suggest some alternative strategies. These strategies are illuminated further through a review of two examples from the recent literature. The paper concludes with a practical overview of the application of these approaches including key decision points and available software.

Censored Variables

Censoring is a property of observed distributions in empirical measures. Using the normal curve as theorized or observed as a benchmark, the censored distribution would look different in at least one important way. With a "normal" variable, a researcher expects to see certain frequency patterns at particular points in the standardized distribution—regardless of the measure's original metric. For example, 95% of the observations will be within at least two standard deviations of the mean, whether above or below. This leaves relatively few cases in either of the thin tails that extend outward along the *X*-axis. In contrast, in a censored distribution there is a heavy concentration of measured responses at the end of at least one of the tails. The observed measure is said to have lower censoring if that concentration is at the bottom of the distribution and upper censoring should the accumulation come at the top. The inherent limiting of variation in the dependent variable due to the censoring means that the true relationship between covariates and the outcome will not be appropriately estimated in classic linear regression (Chay and Powell 2001). In general, as this disproportionate concentration increases it has a greater effect on the observed estimates (Sigelman and Zeng 1999).

This censoring problem comes up in a variety of different areas within broader research on crime and justice (see Figure 1 for illustrative censored distributions). A prominent example is the length of a prison sentence where, in a general sample of criminal cases, a number of offenders receive sentences that do not result in incarceration. This in turn leads to a concentration of

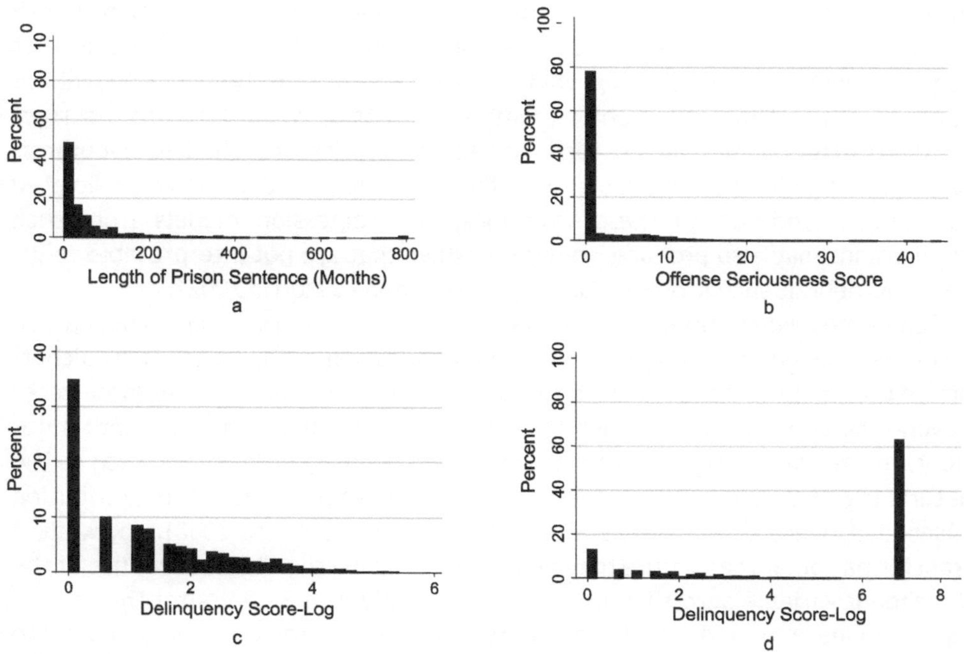

Figure 1 Illustrative censored distributions in crime and justice measures.

observed values at zero, which creates a "floor" effect (see Albonetti 1997; Helms and Jacobs 2002; Nienstedt, Zatz, and Epperlein 1988; Rhodes 1991). Beyond sentencing outcomes, a variety of crime-related measures are affected by this problem, including self-reports of delinquent and criminal behavior (Esbensen and Osgood 1999; Haynie and Osgood 2005; Ousey and Wilcox 2007; Wright, Caspi, Moffitt, and Paternoster 2004), the prevalence and incidence of offending (Nagin and Smith 1990; Paternoster and Triplett 1988; Piquero, Farrington, and Blumstein 2003; Smith, Visher, and Jarjoura 1991), perceptions of risk and intentions to offend (Matsueda, Kreager, and Huizinga 2006; Nagin and Paternoster 1993; Piquero and Pogarsky 2002; Pogarsky and Piquero 2003), inmate misconduct (Gaes and McGuire 1985; Innes 1997), inmate suicide/death (Wooldredge and Winfree 1992), and intimate partner homicide (Dugan, Nagin, and Rosenfeld 1999). In addition to these variables, which typically are censored at the lower portion of their distributions, there are cases where a "ceiling" effect might be observed in the outcome measure. Nagin and Smith (1990), for example, discuss a delinquency scale where, in addition to a number of zero responses, some cases cluster at the upper limit of the distribution as well (see hypothetical distribution in Figure 1d).

Problems and Conventional Solutions

When the values of the dependent variable cluster at a particular point in the distribution (i.e., are censored), they typically do not vary with the covariates in a linear manner, leading to ordinary least squares (OLS) regression coefficients that are misestimated (see Chay and Powell 2001). Use of OLS in that scenario violates the assumption that the error variance in the equation will not vary with the predictor variables (homoskedasticity), which leads to incorrect standard errors that may, in turn, impact conclusions reached in hypothesis testing. Normality assumptions around the regression residuals may be violated as well. In addition to these violations, the regression models from such applications may also produce predicted values that are not interpretable (e.g., negative delinquency scores) (Osgood, Finken, and McMorris 2002).

Sometimes, when this censoring problem is recognized, researchers may transform their dependent variable prior to the application of OLS regression, dichotomize their data and apply logit or probit regression, or analyze only those cases beyond the censoring point. Each of these approaches has some inherent limitations. In the case of data transformation, typically used procedures, such as the natural log, will maintain a cluster of values at a certain point in the distribution (Osgood, Finken, et al. 2002; Sullivan, McGloin, and Piquero 2008). So, while a transformation of that nature may help in normalizing the observed values of the dependent variable across its distribution generally, it does not alter the censoring (see Figure 1c and 1d). Researchers have also expressed doubts about the relative utility of dichotomization of variables when weighed in its totality (MacCallum, Zhang, Preacher, and Rucker 2002). Inherently, this approach results in a loss of information that may be statistically important and substantively useful. MacCallum et al. (2002) report that dichotomization may lead to attenuated effect sizes, spurious significant relationships, and diminished ability to identify non-linear relationships. Discarding the censored cases and analyzing a subset of the original sample are problematic in terms of the general loss of information and these may also have a detrimental impact on the estimates and standard errors in the subsequent analysis (Chay and Powell 2001).

Reflecting on the various distributions shown in the panels in Figure 1 reveals some inherent shortcomings in these approaches. Even if one were to transform these variables, the cases that are presently at the censoring point would remain there. Additionally, collapsing the values beyond the censoring point leads to restricted variance and a loss of information about responses to the outcome variable. Similarly, depending on the degree of censoring in the measure, the use of only the non-censored part of the sample can lead to a considerable loss of information and generalizability and inflated standard errors. For these reasons, preservation of the true range of the measure in conjunction with an alternate model is likely to be preferred to recasting the data using one of these methods.

Censored Regression

Statisticians and econometricians have developed various models to deal with the problems posed by variables that have extreme "floors" or "ceilings" like those mentioned above. The most prominent of these measures is the Tobit regression model, which was originally developed to study household expenditures (Tobin 1958). Spending on some "big ticket" items inherently takes on a non-normal, limited distribution as some households will not spend any money at all on such goods or services in a given time period. The model itself is a hybrid of classic linear regression and probit regression and predicts an underlying continuous version of the observed, but limited, dependent variable. This latent variable is assumed to be normally distributed and the observed censored dependent variable is viewed as a partial representation of its unobserved, continuous counterpart (Long 1997). The model allows for an analysis of dependent variables where the full range of values is not observed (i.e., they are censored at some point) and where a large proportion of observations cluster at the minimum or maximum. The Tobit model is estimated using a maximum likelihood approach (Eliason 1993). Its estimates for the underlying latent variable (y^*) will be consistent if certain assumptions about the model's error terms hold. Specifically, the model assumes that the distribution of conditional errors for the latent variable y^* is normal and homoskedastic (Chay and Honoré 1998). Given satisfaction of some key assumptions, the estimates for this model will have the same properties as OLS coefficients (e.g., linear, additive in relation to the underlying variable) (Osgood, Finken, et al. 2002). Still, as in OLS, violations of these conditions may lead to erroneous substantive conclusions (Sullivan et al. 2008).

While the Tobit model considers the covariate effect on the latent variable associated with the observed outcome, a decomposition of that estimate allows the researcher to (1) assess the effect of each covariate on the probability of being non-censored and (2) attain a second component representing a linear regression coefficient that conditions on a case being above the censoring threshold (i.e., the covariate's linear relationship with the uncensored case) (McDonald and Moffitt 1980; Roncek 1992). Consequently, it is possible to obtain multiple pieces of information that may be relevant to substantive questions of interest—given the sometimes unwieldy interpretation of estimates associated with latent outcome variables. These decomposed effects are also consistent with key substantive questions regarding criminal behavior and justice response. For example, it is useful to know how increases in negative peer influence might impact the probability that a youth will offend and also the degree of that impact on the extent of their offending should they do so. Similarly, it is useful to understand the relationship between key predictors and the likelihood of being imprisoned as well as the length of the sentence should that materialize.

Applications

As highlighted above, there are a number of research areas in crime and criminal justice where censored variables may be identified. We highlight examples from two recent studies to illustrate the context that typically surrounds the use of censored regression models and also consider the manner in which such analyses might be carried out.

Juvenile Delinquency

Information derived from self-report surveys of offending, particularly in general populations, constitutes a source of censored data. Survey respondents frequently report that they have not committed an offense. Consequently, "0" is a common value and measures of offending result in highly skewed distributions. Osgood, Finken, et al. (2002) analyzed the utility of Tobit regression models within the context of multiple-item surveys measuring juvenile delinquency. Data were drawn from the Monitoring the Future study, which consisted of a 14-item self-report survey measuring delinquency among high school seniors.

The authors first identified some of the potential limitations of using OLS methods with these data. Their evaluation of the match of self-report measures to the assumptions of OLS regression suggested that transforming the data to reduce skewness produces a better correspondence between the model and data. Some discrepancies remained, however. Consequently, Item Response Theory (IRT) methods were used to transform the self-reported delinquency scores. This method produces a distribution that more closely resembles the normal curve and reduces skew. Still, this approach does not entirely eliminate the discrepancies between the fitted and observed values in OLS. Typically, IRT characterizes the scores of respondents who reported committing none of the offenses as undefined, leaving questions regarding the cases that fall in the lower bounds of the distribution. Osgood, Finken, et al. (2002) conducted separate analyses to test the utility of OLS and Tobit regressions with self-reported offending. The first analysis consisted of an OLS regression with an untransformed sum of the self-reported items. The second analysis replaced the summative scores with those derived from the IRT model. The third analysis was a Tobit regression of the IRT scores. Based on the findings of previous research, the authors used three common predictors of delinquency to compare the alternative models: sex, sensation seeking, and frequency of unsupervised socializing with peers. They also considered two substantively relevant configurations of regressor-outcome relationships: presence of curvilinear trends and interactive effects.

Their assessment identified some discrepancies in observed means and model predicted values for both OLS equations (with IRT scores and without). Evaluation of the model residuals against their expected values under a constant variance condition revealed that the prediction errors varied systematically with the covariates in both OLS specifications, violating a key assumption. Conversely, the Tobit model showed a strong fit between the actual residuals and those expected under model assumptions. Ultimately, the results revealed that Tobit regression is a more appropriate fit to the data as compared to either OLS approach. Osgood and colleagues' assessment reaffirmed that Tobit regression is particularly useful when measuring the outcomes of self-reported delinquency primarily because it is responsive to the floor effect often observed in such measures. They also demonstrate the importance of considering the censoring problem in the estimation of interactive or curvilinear relationships (see also Ousey and Wilcox 2007).

Prison Sentences

Criminal sentences, scaled by some time unit (years, months), can be a useful outcome measure in considering the effects of various legal and extralegal factors on sanctions delivered by the justice system. In a full sample of cases, however, this variable may be censored due to the fact that some defendants will not receive any formal prison time (i.e., will receive "0" years). Sullivan et al. (2008) studied the effects of modeling choices on the estimated relationship between several legal and extralegal factors (e.g., criminal history, age, and race) and sentence length in U.S. Sentencing Commission Data. The previous literature and study sample suggested the possibility of a heavy concentration of zero values in the sentence length variable, indicating that a censored outcome measure should be expected.

Descriptive analysis revealed that roughly 25% of the cases in the sample had values of zero, reflecting offenders who received no prison time. As in the sentence variable presented in Figure 1, cases beyond the zero point reflect the length of the prison sentence. The distribution was positively skewed beyond the censoring point with various plots and tests suggesting a lack of normality and the potential for non-constant error variance. Although the two models estimate slightly different outcomes (i.e., observed vs. latent variables), these analyses found that OLS and Tobit estimates were generally consistent with respect to the direction of effects. Age and race (White/non-White) had negative effects on length of sentence where older offenders and Whites tended to receive fewer months in prison. Also, predicted sentence length was greater in situations where the criminal history was more extensive. The authors considered decomposed Tobit estimates to highlight key substantive points. For example, although the effect of race was statistically significant, decomposition of the estimate suggested a modest impact on the probability of incarceration (i.e., being censored or not) where Whites were 2% less likely to receive a prison sentence than non-Whites. The magnitude of the estimates was quite different and, consequently, the hypothesis tests led to different conclusions in OLS and Tobit for one of the six variables (age). There was some divergence in comparing those models to more robust censored model estimates as well. Further consideration of the relative strength of the effects suggested that some conclusions might change as a result of model choice (Sullivan et al. 2008).

Working with Censored Variables

These examples, and the discussion preceding them, suggest that it is important to consider the assumptions underlying regression models and evaluate their effects on study conclusions in situations where censoring may be present. The assorted problems of real-world data dictate that statistical practice inevitably diverges somewhat from the underlying theory (Leamer 1978). This requires that the modeling process should subscribe to certain conventions and rules to ensure that subjective decisions do not override the tools being used in a way that unduly impacts the observed estimates.

While there are no absolute rules in dealing with the problems described above, a few guiding principles can be observed (see Figure 2). First, as in any statistical application, understanding the substantive properties of the object of explanation (dependent variable), and its accompanying context, is essential. Certain combinations of samples and measures often imply observed variables with censored distributions. For example, as noted above, summative delinquency scores utilized in general population samples are likely to encounter floor effects as many youth will respond that they have not committed any form of delinquency. A similar scenario is observed in looking at a general sample of convicted offenders in terms of their length of sentence. Second, attention to basic descriptive results will likely reveal a potential censoring problem in the form of a heavy concentration of values at one point in a histogram or frequency distribution. This can often be anticipated, but there may be scenarios where censoring is only revealed through formal inspection of the descriptive results. If OLS regression is applied in a case where censoring is suspected, it is important that the potential violations highlighted above are thoroughly assessed by visual inspection of residuals and formal model specification tests.

If the three previous steps suggest that OLS regression is inappropriate or problematic, a censored regression model as described above and highlighted in the examples may be utilized. In this process it is important to consider that censored regression models also make some assumptions, so there are important costs and benefits to be considered in model choice. Some have suggested that improper use of available alternatives might cause problems that outweigh those that come from applying OLS with censored data (Chay and Powell 2001; Nelson 1981). In such cases, there may be a need to rescale the distribution of non-censored cases (e.g., Osgood, Finken, et al. 2002) and/or utilize a censored regression model that makes fewer assumptions than Tobit (e.g., Sullivan et al. 2008). The interpretation of the covariate effect changes somewhat with a Tobit model as well, so various means of decomposition and elaboration on the estimates may be employed to provide clearer answers to substantive questions. Overall, a thorough consideration of the potential alternatives and their respective rationales is important in ensuring the trustworthiness of the results that emerge in studying sometimes difficult dependent variables. With a clear understanding of their various assumptions, multiple models can be run in order to check the sensitivity of observed findings to potential slippage between statistical expectations and the realities of the observed data (Manski 2007).

The application of the censored regression approaches described here has greatly benefitted from growth in available software and the computing power that allows for intensive estimation procedures to be done relatively effi-

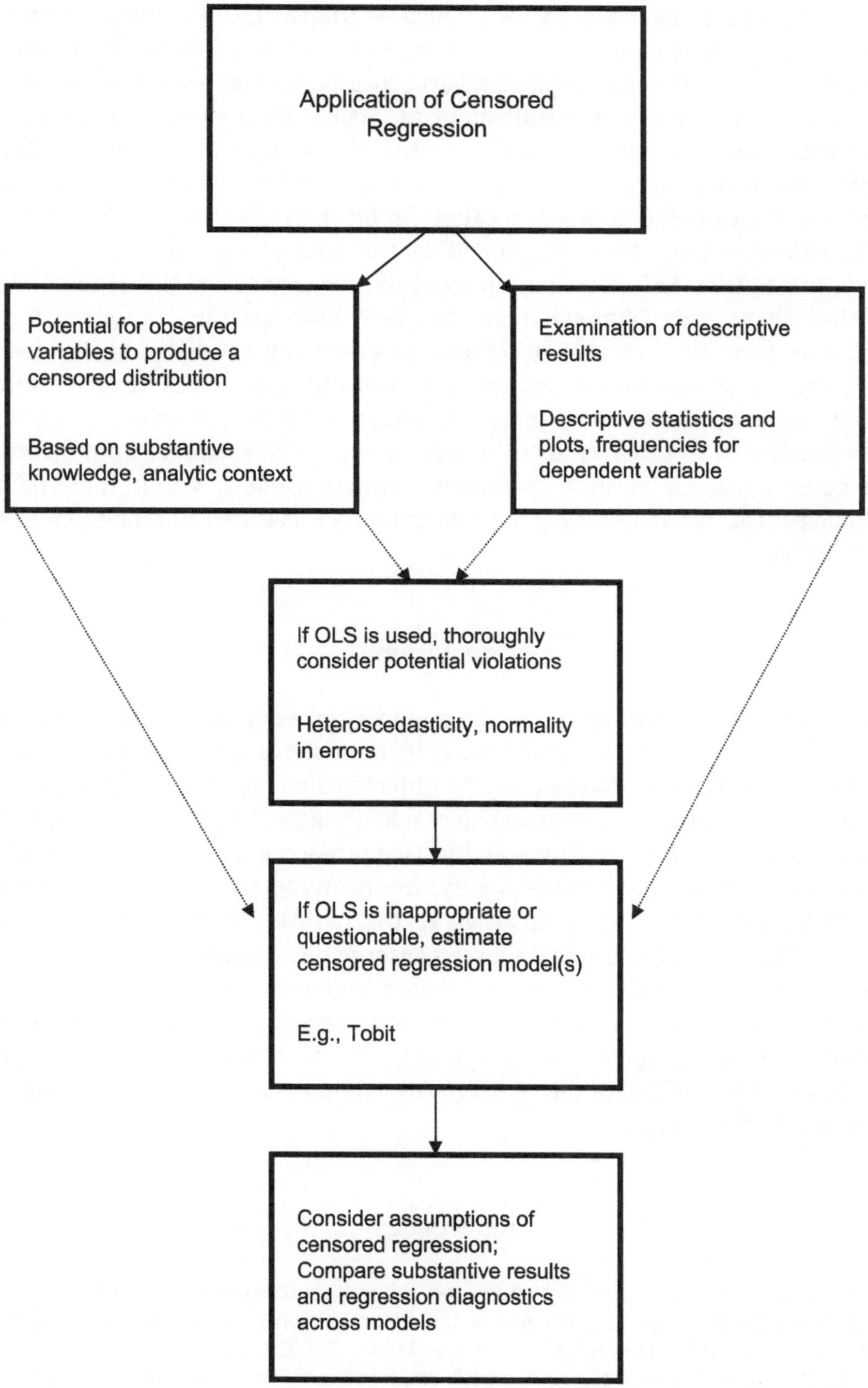

Figure 2 Summary of decision rules and analytic process: censored regression.

ciently. In addition to some relatively straightforward textbook treatments (e.g., Long 1997), software packages such as STATA, LIMDEP, MPlus, and SAS have the capacity to estimate censored regression models such as Tobit. STATA offers command files for running standard censored normal regression as well as a variety of alternatives (see Sullivan et al. 2008). Through its user-generated programs, it also provides alternative means of framing the estimates of Tobit models that researchers might find useful in best addressing their substantive questions. For example, a program called *Dtobit* in STATA provides decomposed Tobit estimates like those mentioned in the sentencing example described above. In addition, SAS offers multiple options for conducting this type of analysis through its *Proc Qlim* command set. SPSS now has the capability to run Tobit regression through user-developed programming as well. This relatively new option is accessible through the SPSS website in the "developer central" area. MPlus and SAS allow the analyst to utilize censored outcome distributions in conjunction with other types of models as well. For example, both incorporate censored variables into longitudinal growth models, which is useful as offending measures may follow such distributions (Muthén and Muthén 2008; Nagin 2005).

Conclusion

In pursuing greater understanding of criminal behavior and justice decision-making, it is essential that researchers craft the right questions and utilize data collection strategies appropriate to the objectives inherent in those questions. Beyond that, sound conclusions must be reached in assessing the information that emerges from that process. Crime and justice researchers are heavily trained in regression techniques, and consequently, frequently apply them. It is important that these applications are responsive to the realities of the observed data, however. Those data frequently follow a censored distribution where values cluster at either end of the distribution, sometimes leading to violations in key assumptions of standard regression models. Censored regression offers one potential solution that, when appropriately applied, allows researchers to more aptly analyze the real world data that emerge from theoretical and applied studies of crime and justice issues.

References

Albonetti, C. A. 1997. Sentencing under the federal sentencing guidelines: Effects of defendant characteristics, guilty pleas, and departures on sentence outcomes for drug offenses, 1991-1992. *Law & Society Review* 31 (4): 789-822.

Berk, R. 2004. *Regression analysis: A constructive critique*. Thousand Oaks, CA: Sage.

Chay, K. Y., and B. E. Honoré. 1998. Estimation of semiparametric censored regression models: An application to changes in black-white earnings inequality during the 1960s. *Journal of Human Resources* 33 (1): 4-38.

Chay, K. Y., and J. L. Powell. 2001. Semiparametric censored regression models. *Journal of Economic Perspectives* 15 (4): 29-42.

Dugan, L., D. Nagin, and R. Rosenfeld. 1999. Explaining the decline in intimate partner homicide: The effects of changing domesticity, women's status, and domestic violence resources. *Homicide Studies* 3 (3): 187-214.

Eliason, S. 1993. *Maximum likelihood estimation: Logic and practice*. Newbury Park, CA: Sage.

Esbensen, F. A., and D. W. Osgood. 1999. Gang Resistance Education and Training (GREAT): Results from the national evaluation. *Journal of Research in Crime & Delinquency* 36 (2): 194-225.

Gaes, G. G., and W. J. McGuire. 1985. Prison violence: The contribution of crowding versus other determinants of prison assault rates. *Journal of Research in Crime & Delinquency* 22 (1): 41-65.

Gottfredson, M. R., and T. Hirschi. 2003. Self-control and opportunity. In C. L. Britt and M. R. Gottfredson (Eds.), *Control theories of crime and delinquency: Advances in criminological theory* (Vol. 12, pp. 5-20). New Brunswick, NJ: Transaction.

Hay, C., and W. Forrest. 2008. Self-control theory and the concept of opportunity: The case for a more systematic union. *Criminology* 46 (4): 1039-1072.

Haynie, D. L., and D. W. Osgood. 2005. Reconsidering peers and delinquency: How do peers matter? *Social Forces* 84 (2): 1109-1130.

Helms, R., and D. Jacobs. 2002. The political context of sentencing: An analysis of community and individual characteristics. *Social Forces* 81 (2): 577-604.

Innes, C. A. 1997. Patterns of misconduct in the federal prison system. *Criminal Justice Review* 22 (2): 157-174.

Leamer, E. E. 1978. *Specification searches: Ad hoc inference with nonexperimental data*. New York: John Wiley.

Long, J. S. 1997. *Regression models for categorical and limited dependent variables*. Thousand Oaks, CA: Sage.

MacCallum, R. C., S. Zhang, K. J. Preacher, and D. D. Rucker. 2002. On the practice of dichotomization of quantitative variables. *Psychological Methods* 7 (1): 19-40.

Manski, C. F. 2007. *Identification for prediction and decision*. Cambridge, MA: Harvard University Press.

Matsueda, R. L., D. A. Kreager, and D. Huizinga. 2006. Deterring delinquents: A rational choice model of theft and violence. *American Sociological Review* 71 (1): 95-122.

McDonald, J. F., and R. A. Moffitt. 1980. The uses of Tobit analysis. *Review of Economics and Statistics* 62 (2): 318-321.

Muthén, L., and B. Muthén. 2008. *MPlus user's guide 5.0*. Los Angeles, CA: Muthén and Muthén.

Nagin, D. S. 2005. *Group based modeling of development*. Cambridge, MA: Harvard University Press.

Nagin, D. S., and R. Paternoster. 1993. Enduring individual differences and rational choice theories of crime. *Law & Society Review* 27 (3): 467-496.

Nagin, D. S., and D. A. Smith. 1990. Participation in and frequency of delinquent behavior: A test for structural differences. *Journal of Quantitative Criminology* 6 (4): 335-356.

Nelson, F. D. 1981. A test for misspecification in the censored normal model. *Econometrica* 49 (5): 1317-1329.

Nienstedt, B. C., M. Zatz, and T. Epperlein. 1988. Court processing and sentencing of drinking drivers: Using new methodologies. *Journal of Quantitative Criminology* 4 (1): 39-59.

Osgood, D. W., L. W. Finken, and B. McMorris. 2002. Analyzing multiple-item measures of crime and deviance II: Tobit regression analysis of transformed scores. *Journal of Quantitative Criminology* 18 (4): 319-347.

Osgood, D. W., B. McMorris, and M. T. Potenza. 2002. Analyzing multiple-item measures of crime and deviance I: Item response theory scaling. *Journal of Quantitative Criminology* 18 (3): 267-296.

Ousey, G. C., and P. Wilcox. 2007. The interaction of antisocial propensity and life-course varying predictors of delinquent behavior: Differences by method of estimation and implications for theory. *Criminology* 45 (2): 401-442.

Paternoster, R., and R. Triplett. 1988. Disaggregating self-reported delinquency and its implications for theory. *Criminology* 26 (4): 591-625.

Piquero, A. R., D. P. Farrington, and A. Blumstein. 2003. The criminal career paradigm: Background and recent developments. In M. Tonry (Ed.), *Crime and justice: Vol. 30. A review of research* (pp. 359-506). Chicago: University of Chicago Press.

Piquero, A. R., and G. Pogarsky. 2002. Beyond Stafford and Warr's reconceptualization of deterrence: Personal and vicarious experiences, impulsivity, and offending behavior. *Journal of Research in Crime & Delinquency* 39 (2): 153-186.

Pogarsky, G., and A. R. Piquero. 2003. Can punishment encourage offending? Investigating the "resetting effect." *Journal of Research in Crime & Delinquency* 40 (1): 95-120.

Rhodes, W. 1991. Federal criminal sentencing: Some measurement issues with application to pre-guideline sentencing disparity. *Journal of Criminal Law & Criminology* 81 (4): 1002-1033.

Roncek, D. W. 1992. Learning more from Tobit coefficients: Extending a comparative analysis of political protest. *American Sociological Review* 57 (4): 503-507.

Sigelman, J., and L. Zeng. 1999. Analyzing censored and sample selected data with Tobit and Heckit models. *Political Analysis* 8 (2): 167-182.

Smith, D. A., C. A. Visher, and C. R. Jarjoura. 1991. Dimensions of delinquency: Exploring the correlates of participation, frequency, and persistence delinquent behavior. *Journal of Research in Crime & Delinquency* 28 (1): 6-32.

Sullivan, C. J., and M. G. Maxfield. 2003. Examining paradigmatic development in criminal justice: A content analysis of research methods syllabi in doctoral programs. *Journal of Criminal Justice Education* 14 (2): 269-285.

Sullivan, C. J., J. M. McGloin, and A. R. Piquero. 2008. Modeling the deviant y^* in criminology: An examination of the assumptions of censored normal regression and potential alternatives. *Journal of Quantitative Criminology* 24 (4): 399-421.

Tittle, C. R., D. A. Ward, and H. G. Grasmick. 2003. Self-control and crime/deviance: Cognitive vs. behavioral measures. *Journal of Quantitative Criminology* 19 (4): 333-365.

Tobin, J. 1958. Estimation of relationships for limited dependent variables. *Econometrica* 26 (1): 24-36.

Wooldredge, J. D., and L. T. Winfree. 1992. An aggregate-level study of inmate suicides and deaths due to natural causes in U.S. jails. *Journal of Research in Crime & Delinquency* 29 (4): 466-479.

Wright, B. R. E., A. Caspi, T. E. Moffitt, and R. Paternoster. 2004. Does the perceived risk of punishment deter criminally prone individuals? Rational choice, self-control, and crime. *Journal of Research in Crime & Delinquency* 41 (2): 180-213.

Index

Page numbers in *Italics* represent tables.
Page numbers followed by n represent endnotes.